No More War!

LINUS PAULING

No More War!

Illustrated with Drawings by
ROGER HAYWARD

DODD, MEAD & COMPANY
New York - - - - *1958*

Published, August, 1958
Second printing, September, 1958

Library of Congress Catalog Card Number: 58-11741

PRINTED IN THE UNITED STATES OF AMERICA
BY QUINN & BODEN COMPANY, INC., RAHWAY, N. J.

To

AVA HELEN PAULING

Preface

We of the mid-twentieth century live in a most extraordinary time. We are living through that unique epoch in the history of civilization when war will cease to be the means of settling great world problems. We shall soon enter upon the continuing period of peace, a period when there will be no more war, when disputes between nations will be settled by the application of man's power of reason, by international law.

It is the development of great nuclear weapons that requires that war be given up, for all time. The forces that can destroy the world must not be used.

The development of these great weapons took place only a short while ago—only half a decade ago there occurred the second terrifying metamorphosis, that from the giant of the kiloton nuclear bomb to the megaton monster.

We have had only a few years to contemplate the nature of life in a world of H-bombs and superbombs. The facts about these bombs and the predictions about the nature of nuclear war have become known to the public only recently, and often they have been released in a protecting cloud of reassuring verbiage. But now the facts are at hand, and we can see for ourselves that our own future and the future of the human race depend upon our willingness and ability to cooperate, to work together in a worldwide attack on the great world problems.

This is the message of this book.

LINUS PAULING

Pasadena, California
15 April 1958

Contents

Contents

No More War!

1
The End of War

I believe that there will never again be a great world war, if only the people of the United States and of the rest of the world can be informed in time about the present world situation. I believe that there will never be a war in which the terrible nuclear weapons—atom bombs, hydrogen bombs, superbombs—are used. I believe that the development of these terrible weapons forces us to move into a new period in the history of the world, a period of peace and reason, when world problems are not solved by war or by force, but are solved by the application of man's power of reason, in a way that does justice to all nations and that benefits all people.

I believe that this is what the future holds for the world, but I am sure that it is not going to be easy for the world to achieve this future. We have to work to prevent the catastrophe of a cataclysmic nuclear war, and to find the ways in which world problems can be solved by peaceful and rational methods.

In the past, disputes between groups of human beings have often been settled by war. At first the wars were fought with stones and clubs as weapons, then with spears and swords, and then with bows and arrows. During the last few hundred years they have been fought with guns, and recently with great bombs dropped from airplanes—

blockbusters containing one ton or even ten tons of TNT.

There may in the past have been times when war was a cruel but effective application of the democratic process, when force was on the side of justice. Wars fought with simple weapons were often won by the side with the greater number of warriors.

Now war is different. A great mass of people without nuclear weapons, without airplanes, without ballistic missiles cannot fight successfully against a small group controlling these modern means of waging war.

The American people were successful in their revolt against Great Britain because modern weapons had not yet been developed when the American Revolution broke out.

It is hard for anybody to understand how great a change has taken place in the nature of the world during the past century or two, and especially during the last fifty years. The world has been changed through the discoveries made by scientists. Everything has been changed by these discoveries—the food we eat, the clothes we wear, the methods of controlling disease, the methods of transportation and communication, the conduct of international affairs, the ways of waging war—all are different now from what they were a few decades ago.

Never again will there be the world of William Shakespeare, the world of Benjamin Franklin, the world of Queen Victoria, the world of Woodrow Wilson.

The scientific discoveries that have changed the world are manifold. I think that the greatest of all scientific discoveries, the greatest discovery that has been made since the discovery of the controlled use of fire by prehistoric man, was the discovery of the ways in which the immense

4

stores of energy that are locked up in the nuclei of atoms can be released.

Many scientists contributed to this discovery. Among them we may mention some of the great ones—Pierre and Marie Curie, Albert Einstein, Ernest Rutherford, Niels Bohr, Ernest Lawrence, Frederic and Irene Joliot-Curie, Otto Hahn, Enrico Fermi.

This discovery, by providing power in essentially unlimited quantities for the future world, should lead through its peaceful applications to a great increase in the standards of living of people all over the world.

It is this discovery also that has changed the nature of war in an astounding way.

The Second World War, like earlier wars, was fought with molecular explosives. Trinitrotoluene, TNT, is the one that was most used. TNT can be manufactured by the reaction of nitric and sulfuric acids with the hydrocarbon toluene, which can be obtained from petroleum. It is not very expensive—somewhere around 25 cents a pound. One pound of TNT can do a lot of damage; about the same as one stick of dynamite. It can demolish a small house and kill several people. A one-ton blockbuster, a bomb containing 2000 pounds of TNT, can demolish a large building and may kill a hundred people or more.

During the Second World War many shells and bombs containing TNT and other explosives were fired at or dropped on cities and other targets in the warring countries. The total amount of explosives used in the whole of the Second World War came to about three million tons of TNT.

In this book we shall often refer to the explosive energy of one million tons of TNT. We may call this one megaton. We should remember that three megatons is the equivalent of all the explosives used in the whole of the Second World War.

At the beginning of the Second World War the discoveries in the field of nuclear physics had just reached such a point as to cause a number of scientists to recognize that it might be possible to manufacture immensely powerful bombs involving nuclear reactions, and also to make nuclear power plants.

In March 1939 Enrico Fermi had a conference with representatives of the Navy Department, with the outcome that the Navy expressed interest and asked to be kept informed. In July 1939 Leo Szilard and Eugene Wigner conferred with Einstein, and a little later Einstein, Szilard, and Wigner discussed the matter with Alexander Sachs. Sachs, supported by a letter from Einstein, then explained the situation to President Roosevelt, who appointed a committee, the "Advisory Committee on Uranium," to look into the problem. In December 1941, after receipt of information about progress made independently by the British, the atomic bomb project was initiated, and in a few years the thousands of American, British, French, and other scientists who had been brought together succeeded in developing atomic bombs of two types, the Hiroshima type (fission of uranium-235) and the Nagasaki type (fission of plutonium-239).

At 8:15 A.M. of 6 August 1945 the first atomic bomb used in war was dropped on Hiroshima, a city of about 450,000 people in the western part of Japan. It was Monday, and the people were setting out on their way to work. The bomb was dropped from an American B-29 flying at about 24,000 feet. The B-29 flew away at full speed as the bomb, supported by a parachute, slowly descended. It exploded above the central part of the city, at a height of about 2200 feet. Within a few seconds the blast from the bomb destroyed 60 percent of the city. Many thousands of people were killed by the blast itself or crushed by falling buildings. Many others were killed by burns, caused by the great amount of radiation from the fireball of the bomb, which had a surface temperature greater than that of the sun. Many thousands of people received exposure to ionizing radiation that caused them to die of radiation sickness in a few days.

About 100,000 people were killed by the bomb in Hiroshima and about another 100,000 seriously injured.

On 9 August 1945, three days after the Hiroshima bomb had been dropped, a second atomic bomb was dropped on Japan. It exploded over Nagasaki, a city of about 300,000 population in southern Japan, on the island of Kyushu. This bomb destroyed a large part of the city, killed about 70,000 people, and seriously injured about another 70,000 people.

The Nagasaki and Hiroshima bombs had explosive energy somewhere between 15,000 and 20,000 tons of TNT. Each of them was accordingly about 15,000 or 20,000 times more powerful than a one-ton blockbuster. Each was about 1000 times as powerful as the greatest of the great bombs with conventional explosives used in the Second World War. Each of them killed more than ten thousand times as many people as were killed by the average blockbuster of the Second World War.

It was clear that war had entered into a new period—the period of atomic bombs.

Within a few days Japan had surrendered (14 August 1945). It was evident that no nation could continue to fight against an enemy nation possessing these terrible weapons. I think that the surrender would have come if the bombs had been dropped in the open country, rather than on the cities of Hiroshima and Nagasaki—the power of the great new weapons would have been demonstrated nearly as clearly in this way, without the great loss of life by the women, children and other non-combatants of the two cities.

In the years following the end of the Second World War many people pointed out that a war waged with atom bombs would produce a devastation incomparably greater than that of the Second World War, would kill hundreds of millions of human beings.

Albert Einstein in 1946 said:

A new type of thinking is essential if mankind is to survive and move to higher levels. Today the atomic bomb has altered profoundly the nature of the world as we know it and the human race consequently finds itself in a new habitat to which it must adapt its thinking. Modern war, the bomb, and other discoveries present us with revolutional circumstances. Never before was it possible for one nation to make war on another without sending armies across borders. Now with rockets and atomic bombs no center of population on the earth's surface is secure from surprise destruction in a single attack. Should one rocket with atomic warhead strike Minneapolis, that city would look almost exactly like Nagasaki. Rifle bullets kill men, but atomic bombs kill cities. A tank is a defense against a bullet, but there is no defense in science against a weapon which can destroy civilization.

Our defense is not in armaments, nor in science, nor in going underground. Our defense is in law and order.

Henceforth every nation's foreign policy must be judged at every point by one consideration: Does it lead us to a world of law and order or does it lead us back toward anarchy and death? I do not believe that we can prepare for war and at the same time prepare for a world community. When humanity holds in its hand the weapon with which it can commit suicide, I believe that to put more power into the gun is to increase the probability of disaster.

The world had indeed entered into a new stage of development in 1945, when the atom bombs were dropped on Hiroshima and Nagasaki and the United States began to build up its stockpile of thousands of these terribly destructive weapons, each one capable of destroying a medium-sized city and killing a hundred thousand people.

Albert Einstein was justified in his great apprehension, his fear that the possession of weapons of destruction a thousand times more powerful than the greatest that were ever used before would lead to catastrophe for the world.

And now we have the H-bomb!

Now the United States, the U.S.S.R., and Great Britain have stockpiles of hydrogen bombs and superbombs that are one thousand times more powerful still than the atomic bombs that were dropped on Hiroshima and Nagasaki!

In 1945 the world changed from the period of TNT blockbusters, with war as in the Second World War, when one large bomb could kill ten people or a hundred people, into its second period, the period of the great atomic bombs, each capable of killing one hundred thousand people. In 1952 the world moved into the *third* period, when the bombs became not just one thousand or ten thousand times more powerful than the blockbusters, but *one million* or *ten million* times as powerful—*one thousand times more powerful than the Hiroshima and Nagasaki bombs.*

9

If a war were to break out today, it is probable that one bomb would explode over New York, and kill ten million people. One bomb would explode over London, and kill ten million people. One bomb would explode over Moscow, and kill six million people. One bomb would explode over Leningrad, and kill three million people. One bomb would explode over Chicago, and kill four million people. One bomb would explode over Los Angeles, and kill three million people. And these cities themselves would be smashed flat, over an area ten miles or twenty miles in diameter. The cities and the regions around them would be rendered uninhabitable for years by the deposited radioactivity. The initial attacks in such a war would kill 83 million Americans and seriously injure another 25 million.

The bomb that could destroy the greatest city in the world and kill ten million people is not something imaginary. Bombs of this sort—hydrogen bombs and super-bombs—have been made and have been exploded. Bombs have been tested that have an explosive power as great as 15 megatons—an explosive power equivalent to 15 million tons of TNT, 15 million one-ton blockbusters.

Each one of these bombs is one thousand times more powerful than the Hiroshima bomb or the Nagasaki bomb. Each one of them has an explosive energy five times as great as that of all of the bombs used in the Second World War.

Albert Einstein was apprehensive, fearful, in 1946, when the world had passed into the period of atomic bombs, little nuclear bombs such that each bomb equals one hundred thousand people killed. How much more reason do we have now for fear about the future of the world, now that we have moved into the period of great nuclear weapons, with each bomb equal to as many as ten million people killed!

We are truly forced into abandoning war as the method of solution of world problems, the method of resolution of disputes among nations.

President Eisenhower and other great national leaders have stated that the stockpiles of these terrible nuclear weapons are deterrents—that they will serve as deterrents against aggression, deterrents against war. There is little doubt that the nuclear weapons have been effective in preventing the outbreak of great wars during recent years.

But disputes between nations still need to be settled. In the past, world problems have often been settled by war, sometimes in such a way as to correspond to justice and sometimes to injustice. If the nuclear stockpiles continue to serve effectively as deterrents and to prevent war from breaking out, there still remains the task of solving the great world problems.

It is evident that these problems now need to be settled by the processes of negotiation, arbitration, the formulation and application of a sound system of international law. *We need to begin now to make international agreements.*

I am not alone in this belief. I think that the great majority of the scientists in the world and the great majority of the people in the world believe that there must be no more war, that the great stockpiles of terribly destructive nuclear weapons must not be used, that the time has come for morality and justice to take their proper place of prime importance in the conduct of world affairs, that world problems should be settled by international agreements and the application of international law.

On 13 January 1958 I presented to the United Nations

a petition to which 9235 scientists, of many countries in the world, had subscribed. In this petition we urged that immediate action be taken to effect an international agreement to stop the testing of all nuclear weapons. We pointed out that if testing continues and the possession of the nuclear weapons spreads to additional governments there will be greatly increased danger of outbreak of a cataclysmic nuclear war through the reckless action of some irresponsible national leader. We mentioned also the damage that is being done to the health of human beings all over the world and to the pool of human germ plasm that determines the nature of future generations by the bomb tests, which spread radioactive elements over every part of the world. We mentioned that an international agreement to stop the testing of nuclear bombs now could serve as the first step toward averting the possibility of a nuclear war that would be a catastrophe for all humanity. Our proposal is that we begin now the new era of peace and international law, by making an international agreement to stop the bomb tests.

It is these matters that will be discussed in some detail in the later chapters of this book. Also, in the final chapter a proposal is made about how peace is to be achieved in the world, how the great world problems are to be solved without recourse to war, war that would now lead to catastrophe, to world suicide.

It is proposed that the great world problems be solved in the way that other problems are now solved—by working hard to find their solution—by carrying on *research for peace*. It is proposed that there be set up a great research organization, the World Peace Research Organization, within the structure of the United Nations. This organization should include many scientists, representing all fields of science, and many other specialists, in all fields of knowledge. They would attack world problems by imaginative and original methods, and would work steadily in this attack, year after year.

The time has now come for man's intellect to win out over the brutality, the insanity of war.

2
The Nature of
Nuclear Weapons

Before we discuss nuclear weapons, let us have a look at one of the old-fashioned explosives, TNT.

TNT is the substance trinitrotoluene. It is made by pouring toluene into a mixture of nitric acid and sulfuric acid. Toluene is a liquid something like benzene. It is found in small quantity in some kinds of petroleum and is easily made from the other constituents of petroleum or natural gas.

TNT is a yellow solid crystalline substance with the chemical formula $C_7H_5N_3O_6$. The crystals consist of molecules, each of which is made of seven carbon atoms, five hydrogen atoms, three nitrogen atoms, and six oxygen atoms, which are arranged in space in the way shown in Figure 1. The drawing shown in Figure 1 represents a magnification of 100 million-fold.

This is a great amount of magnification. If we had one pound of TNT in the form of a ball it would be about three inches in diameter. Now if this ball were to be magnified 100 million times, so that each of the molecules of TNT in it would have the size shown in the figure, the

14

ball itself would have become over 5000 miles in diameter, and hence nearly as large as the earth.

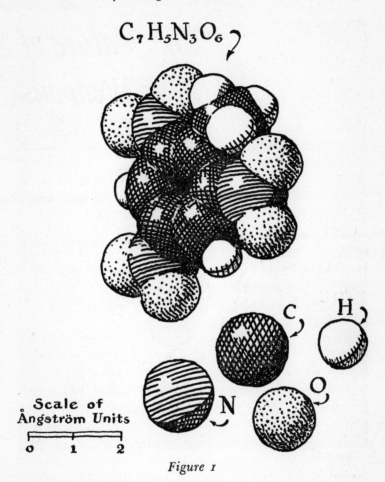

$C_7H_5N_3O_6$

Scale of Ångström Units

0   1   2

Figure 1

When a mass of TNT is detonated by means of a sharp blow, such as that produced by a detonator, the atoms in the molecule separate from one another and unite to form

15

new molecules. These are small molecules, such as shown in Figure 2, where molecules of nitrogen, carbon monox-

Figure 2

ide, and hydrogen are represented. The bonds holding the atoms together in these molecules are stronger than the bonds in the molecule of TNT, and the extra energy that is stored in the bonds of the TNT molecules is released in the explosion. The amount of this energy is such that the products of the explosion reach a temperature of nearly 4000°C.

It is the energy released during the rearrangement of the atoms into new molecules that provides the energy of the TNT explosion. This is the sort of chemical reaction that takes place when a TNT bomb is exploded.

Other molecular explosives, such as nitroglycerin, get their energy from similar chemical reactions. The amount of energy that can be provided by such a molecular explosive is never very much greater than that which is provided by TNT. There is no chance that superbombs can ever be built of molecular explosives.

A molecule such as TNT is made of electrons and atomic nuclei. The electrons and the atomic nuclei are extremely small, over 10,000 times smaller in diameter than the atoms themselves, represented in Figures 1 and 2. Each carbon atom in the TNT molecule has one nucleus. Each atom of hydrogen, nitrogen, and oxygen has one nucleus. These nuclei are not changed at all in the explosion of TNT, nor are the electrons changed; there is only a rearrangement of the atoms during this reaction.

The Hiroshima Bomb

Now let us consider an atomic explosive; for example, uranium-235, which was used in making the Hiroshima bomb.

Uranium-235 is a hard, heavy, white metal. It is nearly as dense as gold: a ball of it three inches in diameter weighs about 10 pounds. Such a ball might constitute the

17

explosive charge of an atomic bomb similar to the Hiroshima bomb.

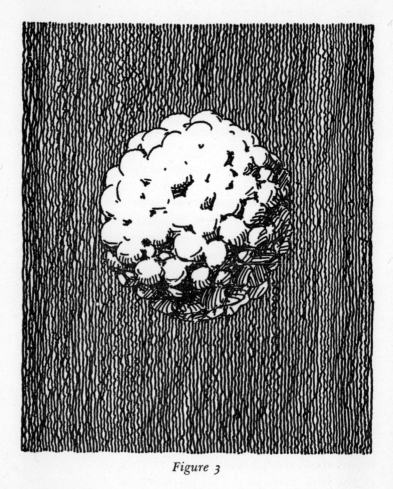

Figure 3

The uranium-235 metal consists of uranium atoms, each of which is a nucleus of uranium-235 surrounded by 92 electrons. When the bomb is exploded it is the uranium-

235 nuclei that react.

In order to make a drawing of the nucleus of uranium-235 we shall need to use a scale of magnification about 50,000 times that used for the molecule of TNT. Such a drawing is shown in Figure 3. It represents a magnification of five million million times; that is, 5,000,000,000,000.

This magnification is truly immense. If we had a ball of uranium-235 weighing 10 pounds, and could enlarge it until the nucleus of each uranium atom had the size shown by the drawing, the ball itself would have become five hundred million miles in diameter. Its diameter would be greater than the distance from the earth to the sun.

The drawing shown in Figure 3 is a somewhat imaginative one. We know a great deal about the molecule of TNT; all of the interatomic distances are known to within about 1 percent, and the drawing shown in Figure 1 is a thoroughly trustworthy one. However, even though the hundreds of physicists who during the last 25 years have been working on the problem of the structure of the atomic nuclei have learned a great deal, they have not yet succeeded in obtaining the sort of detailed information about the structure of the atomic nuclei that has been obtained about the structure of molecules. This is not surprising when we consider that the nuclei are 50,000 times smaller than the molecules—it is one of the marvels of modern science that so much is known about the structure of molecules, and we may have to wait a few years more before similar precise information has been obtained about the nuclei.

The little particles that are represented as forming the nucleus of uranium-235 in Figure 3 are the nucleons. The nucleons are protons and neutrons. It is customary to describe a nucleus of uranium-235 as consisting of 235

19

nucleons of which 92 are protons (particles with a positive charge) and 143 are neutrons (particles with no electric charge). The protons and the neutrons have nearly the same mass; each has a mass approximately $\frac{1}{235}$ of the mass of the uranium-235 nucleus.

The nucleons are held together by forces that in a general sort of way are analogous to, but far stronger than, the forces between atoms that constitute the chemical bonds in the TNT molecule. Under certain circumstances the nucleons may be rearranged, just as the atoms in the molecule of TNT are rearranged during the explosion of TNT.

In the explosion of an atomic bomb this rearrangement occurs after the nucleus has collided with a free neutron.

Reactions of this sort take place all the time in every piece of uranium metal and in every sample of any compound of uranium. There are a few neutrons running around everywhere. A neutron may result, for example, from the collision of a cosmic ray, coming in from outer space, with an atom. If this neutron collides with a nucleus of uranium-235 it may be absorbed by the nucleus, which then contains 236 nucleons, rather than 235—it has become a nucleus of uranium-236. The nucleus of uranium-236 is unstable, in such a way that it spontaneously rearranges, decomposes, as shown in Figure 4. The nucleus splits into two half-sized nuclei, which may be called daughter nuclei. Not all of the nucleons remain in the two daughter nuclei; instead two or three escape as free neutrons. Sometimes the splitting of the uranium-236 nucleus occurs in such a way as to give three daughter nuclei, rather than two, plus a few free neutrons.

In this reaction, which is called the *fission* of the nucleus, a tremendous amount of energy is liberated. The amount of energy liberated by the fission of one uranium nucleus is about ten million times as great as the amount

Figure 4

liberated in the decomposition of one molecule of TNT. The molecule of TNT has about the same weight as the atom of uranium; accordingly the explosive uranium-235

21

is, on a weight basis, about ten million times as powerful as TNT.

A small piece of uranium-235, a few pounds of the metal, will not explode under ordinary conditions. Every once in a while a stray neutron will bump into one of the uranium nuclei and cause it to undergo fission. Two or three neutrons may be liberated in the process of fission, but in general they escape to the surrounding world. Occasionally one of them may hit another uranium nucleus and cause it to undergo fission, too, but the small piece of uranium-235 does not explode.

However, a large piece of uranium-235 is very dangerous—it will explode spontaneously. The size of the piece of the metal that explodes spontaneously is called the *critical mass*. The process that is involved in its spontaneous explosion is called a *chain reaction*.

We may describe the way in which the chain reaction operates. A stray neutron hits a uranium nucleus, perhaps near the center of the piece of uranium-235, and causes it to undergo fission. Let us assume that two neutrons are liberated in the process of fission. If the piece of uranium-235 is a big one, each of these two neutrons will bump into another uranium nucleus, and there will be two more nuclei that undergo fission, and four neutrons will be liberated. These four neutrons will then cause four uranium nuclei to undergo fission, liberating eight neutrons. As this chain reaction continues there will be sixteen, thirty-two, sixty-four, and so on, nuclei undergoing fission, and within a millionth of a second most of the uranium-235 nuclei will have been caused to decompose. This is the process of explosion of the fissionable material of the atomic bombs.

I do not know exactly how the Hiroshima atomic bomb

was built. Perhaps it consisted of two little pieces of uranium-235, each weighing perhaps five pounds, which were held a few inches away from one another in the bomb. There might have been then a couple of pieces of TNT or some similar ordinary explosive on the far sides of the two pieces of uranium-235, such that when they were detonated they would push the two pieces of uranium-235 together, producing a mass greater than the critical mass. Then the chain reaction would begin, and within a millionth of a second the atomic bomb would have exploded— and then within a few seconds many of the hundred thousand victims would be dead.

There is another possibility. Perhaps a mass of, say, ten pounds of uranium-235 is stable under ordinary circumstances, but becomes unstable, so as to explode by the chain reaction, when it is compressed into a smaller volume. The bomb might thus have been made of a ball of uranium-235 about three inches in diameter (perhaps with a central cavity) and weighing about ten pounds, surrounded by some TNT or other molecular explosive with detonators arranged in such a way that when the explosion of the ordinary explosive occurred the ball of uranium-235 would be subjected to great pressure, and be compressed down to two inches in diameter, and this small ball of compressed uranium-235 would then undergo the chain reaction.

The Nagasaki Bomb

The Nagasaki bomb was closely similar to the Hiroshima bomb, but used plutonium-239 as the explosive, in place of uranium-235.

The uranium-235 of the Hiroshima bomb had been

separated from natural uranium metal by a physical process. Natural uranium metal consists almost entirely of the isotope uranium-238; only about 0.7 percent is uranium-235. Uranium-238 cannot be used by itself to make an atomic bomb, nor can natural uranium, the mixture of uranium-238 and uranium-235, be used. Some great plants were built in Oak Ridge to carry out the difficult process of separating the uranium-235 from natural uranium.

A second way of obtaining fissionable material was put into operation in a great plutonium plant in Hanford, Washington. Rods of uranium metal, ordinary uranium, are piled together with rods of graphite, which serves to slow down the neutrons, which are ejected at high speed from the fissioning nuclei. The neutrons that are produced by the fission of uranium-235 are captured by the nuclei of uranium-238, which are then converted into nuclei of uranium-239. The nuclei of uranium-239 decompose spontaneously, with the emission of an electron, to produce nuclei of neptunium-239, and these nuclei soon decompose spontaneously in the same way with the production of nuclei of plutonium-239. The nucleus of plutonium-239 contains 94 protons and 145 neutrons.

Plutonium has chemical properties greatly different from those of uranium, and the plutonium made in this way can be easily separated from the uranium by chemical methods. These methods are so much simpler than the physical methods needed to separate uranium-235 from uranium-238 as to give plutonium an advantage as a fissionable material. In addition, its properties as a nuclear explosive are somewhat superior to those of uranium-235.

Plutonium-239 is a rather stable substance; under ordinary conditions only about half of it has decomposed after 25,000 years. But it is fissionable in the same way as uranium-235. If a mass of plutonium-239 metal is compressed or brought together in such a way as to permit the chain reaction to go on, the plutonium-239 combines with neutrons and undergoes fission to half-size or smaller nuclei, with the liberation of additional free neutrons, and in a small fraction of a second the nuclear explosion has taken place. It was perhaps ten pounds of plutonium-239 made in Hanford that constituted the explosive of the Nagasaki bomb.

It is possible to carry out the explosion of a smaller amount of uranium-235 or plutonium-239; atomic bombs somewhat smaller than the Hiroshima bomb and the Nagasaki bomb have been tested. I do not know just how small the smallest ones are—perhaps about the equivalent of 1000 tons of TNT, involving the fission of an ounce or two of the fissionable metal. A bomb exploded in an underground test in Nevada on 19 September 1957 was stated by a representative of the Atomic Energy Commission to be a 1.7-kiloton bomb—the equivalent of only 1700 tons of TNT.

Also, it is possible to make still larger bombs with uranium-235 or plutonium-239, as large as about 100 kilotons equivalent of TNT. There may be technical difficulties in making these bombs much larger than this.

But the problem of making extremely powerful bombs has been solved. The solution that has been found will be described in the following two sections.

Hydrogen Bombs

Energy is liberated by the decomposition of molecules, such as those of TNT, as we have mentioned at the beginning of this chapter. Also, energy is liberated in some chemical reactions that involve the formation of larger molecules, rather than their decomposition. For example, hydrogen and oxygen burn together to produce water. The hydrogen-oxygen flame is a very intense one, giving a white heat. In this chemical reaction the molecules that react contain only two atoms apiece, and the molecules that are produced, those of water, contain three atoms apiece.

In an analogous way there occur not only nuclear reactions in which large nuclei decompose into smaller ones, by fission, but also nuclear reactions in which larger nuclei are formed from smaller ones. This process is called *fusion*. Fusion and fission are the two kinds of nuclear reactions that are used in nuclear weapons.

Perhaps the most important fusion reaction that takes place is the reaction of hydrogen nuclei (protons) to form helium nuclei (made of four nucleons—two protons and two neutrons). This reaction takes place, in a rather complicated way, in the interior of the sun. It is this fusion process that provides the energy that is radiated by the sun, and that has kept the sun hot for billions of years. The fusion reaction of hydrogen nuclei to form helium nuclei liberates about 50 million times as much energy as is liberated by the reaction of the same weight of hydrogen molecules and oxygen molecules to form water molecules.

There are various difficulties in making hydrogen bombs—bombs that use nuclear fusion for the major part of their explosive energy. However, these difficulties were overcome at about the same time, five years ago, by the American bomb-makers and the Russian bomb-makers; and about one year ago (1957) the British bomb-makers, too, exploded some hydrogen bombs.

The atomic nuclei have a positive electric charge. Two particles with a positive electric charge repel one another, and hence under ordinary conditions two protons, for example, will not get close enough to one another to undergo nuclear reaction. At extremely high temperatures, of the order of 50 million degrees centigrade, the nuclei have so much energy of translational motion—they are moving so rapidly around—that they are able to collide with one another effectively and to undergo reaction. Fusion reactions can accordingly be made to take place by providing a way of heating the reaction materials to about 50 million degrees.

So far the success of the hydrogen-bomb program has depended upon a method of obtaining temperatures of about 50 million degrees that has been at hand since 1945: when an atomic bomb of the Hiroshima type or the Nagasaki type explodes it produces a body of hot gas with temperature about 50 million degrees.

A hydrogen bomb is made by starting with an ordinary atomic bomb, in which the fission process of uranium-235 or plutonium-239 takes place. This atomic bomb acts as the detonator for the fusion process. It heats the hydrogen nuclei or other light nuclei that are to undergo fusion to a very high temperature, so that some of them collide with one another and react, liberating great amounts of fusion energy. The temperature may become even higher as a result of the fusion process, and more of the fusionable material may then react.

If a few pounds of the fissionable material is used as a detonator, and it is surrounded by several hundred pounds or even a ton or two of fusionable material, a hydrogen bomb can be made. Such a bomb is not much greater in

27

weight than a one-ton TNT blockbuster of the good old days of molecular explosives, but it has an explosive energy 10 million or 20 million times that of the one-ton blockbuster, one thousand times as great as that of a Hiroshima or Nagasaki bomb.

There may be no limit to the size of such a hydrogen bomb. So far as I know, the biggest ones that have been tested have been in the range of five to ten megatons— that is, each one of them equivalent to twice or three times all of the bombs exploded in the Second World War. Perhaps the principal reason for not making them any bigger is that there is no target in the world that requires a bomb much bigger than ten megatons.

Ordinary hydrogen, with a proton as the nucleus of its atoms, is not the principal material used in hydrogen bombs. There are two heavier isotopes of hydrogen. One of these is deuterium, which has a nucleus made of two nucleons, a proton and a neutron. This heavy hydrogen was discovered by Professor Harold C. Urey and his collaborators about twenty-five years ago. Another isotope of hydrogen is tritium. Tritium has mass three—its nucleus consists of a proton and two neutrons. The tritium nucleus is unstable, and tritium does not occur in significant amount in nature. It can, however, be made by the use of neutrons from a nuclear reactor.

A hydrogen bomb probably could be constructed with the use of a mixture of deuterium and tritium, plus, of course, the ordinary atomic bomb as its detonator. However, elementary deuterium and tritium, like ordinary hydrogen, are gases at room temperature and atmospheric pressure, and it would be quite inconvenient to have to liquefy these gases and to keep the hydrogen bomb at an extremely low temperature, close to the absolute zero, until it was exploded. A nuclear device of this sort, weighing 60 tons, was detonated for the first time by the U.S. in the autumn of 1952. It yielded energy equivalent to 5 megatons of TNT.

It is likely that in all hydrogen bombs in the U.S., U.S.S.R., and British stockpiles use is made of a compound containing lithium. Lithium and hydrogen form the compound lithium hydride, which is a solid substance under ordinary conditions, and stable so long as it does not come into contact with water. Lithium deuteride is a similar solid substance. A hydrogen bomb can be made by putting a thousand pounds of lithium deuteride around an ordinary atomic bomb, the detonator. Such a bomb was first detonated by the U.S.S.R., in August 1953.

Also, the isotope of lithium that contains six nucleons reacts with a neutron to produce helium and tritium, and the tritium produced in this way can then react with the deuterium to produce more helium, liberating additional neutrons. Deuterium can be made in unlimited amounts by fractionating ordinary water. Lithium can be obtained in unlimited amounts from the ores of lithium, such as lepidolite. Hydrogen bombs probably can be made very cheaply.

Superbombs

Hydrogen bombs sound like the answer to the generals' prayer—they are cheap, they can be made from rather easily available materials in unlimited number, and they can be made as big as desired, big enough to take care of any target in the world.

Nevertheless, it has been found possible to do still better. Superbombs are even cheaper, and they can do anything that a hydrogen bomb can do and something else besides.

In the process of making uranium-235 or of making plutonium-239, ordinary uranium is depleted of its uranium-235. The residue, uranium-238, was for a while a drug on the market. There was no use to which it could be put.

It cannot be used to make an ordinary atomic bomb. However, it will undergo fission under the conditions of extremely high temperatures that exist when a hydrogen bomb is detonated.

It is accordingly possible to convert a hydrogen bomb into a superbomb in a simple way: by surrounding it with a shell of uranium-238 metal (or of ordinary uranium metal, uranium-238 containing a small amount of uranium-235). In this way the explosive power of the bomb may be doubled or tripled at little additional cost. And, moreover, the uranium-238, when it undergoes fission, produces great amounts of radioactive fission products, which may be effective in killing off additional millions of people in the enemy country.

The superbomb is a fission-fusion-fission bomb. When a superbomb is detonated the first process that occurs is the fission of a few pounds of uranium-235 or plutonium-239, with the liberation of energy equivalent to 20,000 tons or 100,000 tons of TNT. The temperature is raised to about fifty million degrees, and about a thousand pounds of lithium deuteride may then undergo the fusion reaction, liberating ten megatons TNT equivalent of energy. At this high temperature a thousand pounds of uranium-238 undergoes fission, liberating an additional ten megatons of explosive energy, and also producing a great amount of radioactive fission products.

Several superbombs have been detonated during recent years. It has been estimated that the first superbomb, exploded by the United States at Bikini on 1 March 1954, had a fusion stage of about five megatons and a fission stage, the third stage, of about twelve megatons. The largest Russian superbombs, including those of March 1958, seem to have been of about the same size.

These hydrogen bombs and superbombs are the weapons that will be used in a Third World War, if there ever is such a war. I cannot believe that man is so lacking in intelligence, so lacking in the power of reason, as to permit a Third World War, a great nuclear war, to take place.

Important attributes of the new weapons are their production of great amounts of high-energy radiation at the moment of explosion and also their production of radioactive materials that give rise to high-energy radiation at later times. These attributes add to the present world danger.

In the following chapters of this book various aspects of nuclear weapons and nuclear war will be presented in detail. These include the nature of radioactivity and fallout (Chapter 3) and the effect of fallout on future generations of human beings (Chapter 4) and on the health of human beings now living (Chapter 5), the resolution of apparently contradictory statements about fallout and its biological effects (Chapter 6), the nature of nuclear war (Chapter 7), the appeals for peace that have been made by scientists (Chapter 8), the necessity for international agreements and international law in the peaceful solution of world problems (Chapter 9), and a proposal about research for peace (Chapter 10). Appeals by Albert Einstein and Albert Schweitzer for reason and peace in the world, as well as the Mainau Declaration of Nobel Laureates, are given in the appendixes.

3
Radioactivity and Fallout

Toward the end of the last century some scientists began to think that they had a nearly complete understanding of the nature of the physical world, that they could explain everything that was happening about them. Then, beginning in 1895, there came a period of great discovery—the discovery of a new world, the world of minute particles, the world of x-rays and radioactivity.

The first great discovery leading into this new world was the discovery of x-rays by a German professor of physics, Wilhelm Konrad Roentgen, in 1895. He was experimenting with a glass bulb from which most of the air had been pumped out. There were metal electrodes in the bulb, and he was passing an electric discharge through the bulb. He found that even after he had surrounded the bulb with black paper a fluorescent screen in the neighborhood would emit light while the electric discharge was passing through the bulb. The fluorescent screen was a piece of cardboard coated with a layer of zinc sulfide or some other substance with the property that ultraviolet light (or other radiation that is usually not visible to the eye) that impinges upon it causes the emission of visible light.

Roentgen showed that the radiation coming from his bulb, now called an x-ray tube, could penetrate matter—could pass through the human body. Within a few weeks after the announcement of this great discovery x-rays were being used by physicians for the investigation of patients.

After some years it was shown that x-rays are similar in nature to ordinary visible light, but their wavelength is far smaller, only 1/1000 or 1/10,000 as great as that of visible light.

When an x-ray tube of the type used by Roentgen is operated, the glass of the tube emits a greenish fluorescence. The great French mathematician Henri Poincaré suggested at a meeting of the French Academy of Sciences that the x-radiation might be related in some way to the fluorescence of the glass. This suggestion stimulated the French physicist Henri Becquerel to investigate some fluorescent minerals—minerals that give out visible light when they are illuminated with ultraviolet light. Becquerel was Professor of Physics in the Museum of Natural History in Paris, where his father and grandfather also had held the same post. His father had collected many fluorescent minerals, which were available in the Museum. Becquerel discovered that the minerals containing uranium had the power of emitting radiation that would pass through paper and other materials, in a way somewhat similar to x-rays. This was the discovery of radioactivity, made in 1896.

Then Marie Sklodovska Curie and her husband Professor Pierre Curie began to study ores of uranium in order to find out something about the source of the radioactivity. They dissolved pitchblende, an ore of uranium, in acid, and carried out chemical separation procedures. After two years, in 1898, Madame Curie was able to isolate from the pitchblende a small amount of a new substance, a compound of a new element, a highly radioactive element, which she named polonium. In the same year, 1898, the Curies isolated another new radioactive substance, the chloride of the element that they named radium.

These radioactive substances have most surprising properties. In addition to giving out rays that can penetrate matter, such as the human body, the substances are a source of energy. A sample of a radioactive substance, such as radium chloride, is warmer than the surrounding room, and remains warmer year after year. At first it seemed that the radioactive materials might provide a perpetual source of energy, but it was soon discovered that, in fact, the radioactivity decreases in intensity with the passage of time. In 25 years a sample of radium chloride loses one percent of its activity.

Atoms such as those of the ordinary metal lead last forever, so far as we know. But the atoms of radium do not last forever—after 25 years one percent of them have ceased to be atoms of radium. It was discovered that the atoms of radium change into atoms of the gas radon, and that the atoms of radon in the course of a few days change into atoms of polonium, which then change into atoms of lead.

When it was discovered (in 1911) that every atom has a heavy nucleus, which is surrounded by electrons, it was recognized that the reactions of a radioactive substance are reactions involving the atomic nuclei. A nucleus of radium changes into a nucleus of radon, which then changes into a nucleus of polonium, and so on.

Alpha Rays, Beta Rays, and Gamma Rays

Three kinds of rays, called alpha rays, beta rays, and gamma rays, are emitted by the heavy radioactive elements. Alpha rays and beta rays are fast-moving particles emitted by the decomposing radioactive nuclei. Gamma rays are rays of penetrating radiation, identical in nature with x-rays. When this high-energy radiation is produced by an x-ray tube it is called x-radiation, and when it is produced by the nuclei of atoms during radioactive decay it is called gamma radiation.

The high-energy radiation from radioactive materials is dangerous to life. Many of the early scientists and physicians who worked with x-rays and with radioactive materials received severe burns from the radiation, burns that would not heal and that often had to be treated by amputation of the hands or arms. Others, such as Madame Curie herself and her daughter, Madame Joliot-Curie, have died of a disease (leukemia) that is believed to have been caused by the radiation.

The x-rays and radioactive rays have also, of course, been of great benefit to man. In addition to their use by scientists in the study of the nature of the world, they have been used for diagnosis of disease and for treatment of disease, especially of cancer.

The nucleus of the radium atom can be described as built of 88 protons and 138 neutrons. It decomposes to produce a radon nucleus, which contains 86 protons and 136 neutrons. The decomposition involves the emission of an alpha particle, which shoots out at high speed. The alpha particle, which is a helium nucleus, is a structure composed of two protons and two neutrons.

Although the alpha particle has great energy, it does not penetrate very far through matter. The alpha particles from radium on the surface of the skin or in the bones of a human being penetrate through a distance of only about one fiftieth of an inch into the adjacent or surrounding tissues.

Other radioactive materials emit beta rays. Beta rays are electrons that are shot out of the atomic nucleus at high speed. Radioactive nuclei such as strontium-90 and yttrium-90 emit beta rays that have the power of penetrating about one eighth of an inch through the tissues of the human body.

Also, radioactive nuclei often emit gamma rays. The gamma rays from radioactive nuclei are in general highly penetrating—these rays can pass completely through the human body, irradiating all parts of it, in the same way as x-rays from an x-ray tube operated at very high voltage.

The effects on the human body of the radiation from radioactive materials will be discussed in the following two chapters.

Half-life

The decomposition of a radioactive atomic nucleus has an interesting characteristic—it is a chance event, which cannot be precisely predicted. A radon nucleus freshly formed by decomposition of a radium nucleus does not start out in life in full vigor, gradually get old, and then, after it reaches old age, die with the emission of an alpha particle and conversion into a polonium nucleus. Instead, it has exactly the same chance of decomposing during the first second after its birth from the radium nucleus as it has after the tenth second or after the hundredth second or the thousandth second.

It is found that after a sample of radon has been watched for 3 days 19 hours and 12 minutes half of the radon nuclei have decomposed. After another 3 days 19 hours and 12 minutes half of the remainder have decomposed, and so on. The activity falls off slowly, with half of the remaining nuclei decomposed after each period of time of this length.

This period of time, the time required for half of the nuclei to undergo radioactive decomposition, is called the half-life of the radioactive material.

Radioactive elements differ very much in their half-lives. The half-life of radium is 1600 years—much greater than that of radon. The half-life of the parent element uranium-238 is 4,500,000,000 years. Uranium is accordingly an element whose nuclei are almost but not quite stable against radioactive decomposition. Many other nuclei are completely stable, so far as can be detected. Some radioactive nuclei have very short half-lives, only a small fraction of a second.

An interesting use of radioactivity is the determination of the age of materials containing carbon by measuring their radioactivity due to carbon-14. This technique of radiocarbon dating can be used to permit the determination of the age of the materials, with an accuracy of 100 or 200 years, provided that they are not more than about 40,000 years old (the sensitivity of the technique at the present time is such as to impose this limitation). The age is the time that has gone by since the material (plant or animal) was made from carbon dioxide in the atmosphere. The method was developed by Dr. Willard F. Libby, of the University of Chicago, who has now for several years been one of the Atomic Energy Commissioners.

Ordinary carbon is carbon-12—its nuclei are made of

six protons and six neutrons. The nuclei of radiocarbon, carbon-14, are made of six protons and eight neutrons. Carbon-14 is produced at a steady rate in the upper atmosphere by a reaction of nitrogen nuclei caused by cosmic rays. The atoms of carbon-14 in the course of time combine with oxygen to form carbon dioxide, and the carbon dioxide, radioactive and non-radioactive alike, is absorbed by plants, which build the carbon atoms into their tissues. Animals that eat the plants also build the carbon atoms into their tissues.

Just after a plant or animal dies the amount of radioactivity of the carbon in its tissues is determined by the amount of carbon-14 in its tissues, which is the standard amount corresponding to the amount of carbon-14 in the atmosphere. However, the half-life of carbon-14 is 5568 years, and accordingly after 5568 years half of the carbon-14 has undergone decomposition, and the radioactivity of the material is only half as great as it was originally. After 11,136 years only one-quarter of the original radioactivity is left, and so on. Thus, by determining the radioactivity of a sample of carbon from wood, flesh, charcoal, skin, horn, bone, or other plant or animal remains, the number of years that have gone by since the carbon was originally extracted from the atmosphere can be determined.

Some thousands of samples have been dated in this way, with very interesting results. For example, the eruption of Mount Mazama in southern Oregon, which formed the crater now called Crater Lake, was determined to have occurred 6453 ± 250 years ago by the dating of charcoal from a tree killed by the eruption. Several pairs of woven rope sandals found in some caves in southern Oregon that had been covered by an earlier eruption were found to be 9050 ± 350 years old. Charcoal from campfires in the

Lascaux Cave near Montignac, France, which contains some remarkable paintings made by prehistoric man, were found to be 15,500 years old.

It is unfortunate that the bomb tests have caused the concentration of carbon-14 in the atmosphere to increase by about 10 percent, and it now continues to increase at the rate of 2 or 3 percent per year. In consequence, the dating of materials by the carbon-14 method in future millennia will be uncertain.

Units of Measurement of Radiation

In this book, in discussing all kinds of high-energy radiation we shall make use of the unit of measurement called the *roentgen* or *roentgen unit*.

All high-energy radiation—alpha rays, beta rays, gamma rays, x-rays—produces ions when it passes through matter. The number of ions produced depends on the quantity of radiation and upon its nature. The ions are produced by the interaction of the radiation with atoms or molecules; electrons are knocked out of the atoms or molecules, leaving the atoms or molecules with a positive electric charge —these electrically charged atoms or molecules are called ions.

The roentgen is defined as the amount of radiation that produces a certain number of ions when it passes through a cubic centimeter of air.

The biological effects of high-energy radiation seem to be produced in large part by the power of the radiation to produce ions, and accordingly these biological effects are pretty well represented quantitatively by the roentgen as a unit of measurement of the radiation.

The *curie* is the unit of radioactivity. It is defined as the

39

quantity of radioactive material in which 37,000,000,000 atomic nuclei disintegrate each second. One gram of radium has the activity of one curie.

The *millicurie* is one one-thousandth of a curie. The *microcurie* is one one-millionth of a curie. The *micromicrocurie* is one one-millionth of a millionth of a curie.

In the discussion of fallout we shall make use of the *strontium unit* and the *cesium unit*. The strontium unit is a measure of the amount of radioactive strontium (strontium-90) in human bone or milk or other material containing calcium. One strontium unit is one micromicrocurie of strontium-90 per gram of calcium. One cesium unit is one micromicrocurie of cesium-137 per gram of potassium.

Everybody is exposed to high-energy radiation from natural sources. Part of the exposure is from natural radioactive nuclei, the principal ones being radium, radon, potassium-40, and carbon-14. These radioactive nuclei are present in the rocks, air (radon and carbon-14), and other materials surrounding us, and are also present inside the human body.

Another part of the radiation comes from cosmic rays. Cosmic rays are particles of very high energy that reach the earth from interstellar space or other parts of the universe, or are produced in the earth's atmosphere by the rays from outer space. The discovery that ionizing radiation reaches the earth's surface from outer space was made by the Austrian physicist Victor Hess, who made measurements of ionization during balloon ascents in 1911 and 1912. The cosmic rays that impinge on the outer parts of the earth's atmosphere consist of protons and the nuclei of heavier atoms moving with very great speeds. The cosmic rays that reach the surface of the earth consist in large part of smaller particles and high-energy radiation produced by reaction of the original heavier particles with the atomic nuclei in the earth's atmosphere.

Two sets of estimates of the amount of natural background radiation to which human beings are subjected, on the average, are given in Table 1. The first of these sets is due to Dr. W. F. Libby (page 1459 of *The Nature of Radioactive Fallout and Its Effects on Man*). It may be considered to be the official estimate of the AEC. The second estimate is that of the report of the British Medical Research Council to the British Parliament, June 1956, "The Hazards to Man of Nuclear and Allied Radiations";

Table 1

Estimated Dose Rate to Gonads from Natural Sources of Radiation

Radiation source	Estimated average dose rate to gonads in roentgens per year	
	Libby	British Report
External radiation:		
Cosmic rays (sea level)	0.033 to 0.037	0.028
Gamma rays from the earth	0.020 to 0.110	0.043
Radon in air		0.001
Internal radiation:		
Potassium-40	0.019	0.020
Carbon-14	0.002	0.001
Radium, radon and decay products	0.007 *	0.002
Total	0.081 to 0.175	0.095

* Exposure of bones only.

41

it is found on page 1590 of *The Nature of Radioactive Fallout and Its Effects on Man.*

The range of values given by Libby is due in small part to a geographical effect of the cosmic rays, and in large part to the nature of the environment. The minimum values correspond to being on the open ocean and the maximum values to being surrounded by ordinary granite. The values for being surrounded by typical sedimentary rock are given by Libby as about 0.023 greater than for the open ocean. They correspond reasonably well with the British estimate.

There is some increase in cosmic ray intensity with altitude. Most of the people in the world live at sufficiently low altitudes that it is not necessary to take this fact into consideration in discussing the average exposure.

Another estimate of the average dose rate to the gonads from natural sources is 0.110 roentgens per year, made by Dr. Robert A. Dudley and Dr. Robley D. Evans of the Massachusetts Institute of Technology (*The Nature of Radioactive Fallout and Its Effects on Man,* page 1240). This is a reasonable average of the values given in Table 1, and in the remainder of this book we shall assume that the average dosage of radiation to which people throughout the world are exposed from natural sources is about 0.110 roentgens per year. This amounts to 3.3 roentgens in 30 years.

Some people in the world receive radiation exposures from other sources. Everybody in the world is now receiving some additional exposure from fallout from the atomic bomb tests. In addition, many people are given x-ray treatment for diagnostic or therapeutic purposes. The Committee on Biological Effects of Atomic Radiation of the National Academy of Sciences-National Research

Council estimated that the average exposure of people in the United States to medical x-rays at the present time is about 3 roentgens in thirty years—that is, roughly equal to the average exposure to natural radiation. In many other parts of the world the exposure to x-rays is considerably smaller, and it seems likely that, now that the danger of exposure to x-rays has been strongly emphasized in recent years, the average exposure in the United States will decrease significantly in the future.

Of course, it must be remembered that the use of x-rays in medical practice is of great value, and that the danger of genetic and somatic damage by the x-rays is one that often must be taken, although it should be kept to a minimum by taking care that the x-ray exposure is not made except when necessary and then not in amounts greater than necessary.

There are also some workers who are exposed to ionizing radiation in the course of their work, as, for example, in the peacetime applications of atomic energy. The problem of minimizing the damage to the health of human beings and to future generations of human beings done by radiation from these sources is an important one, which will have to be attacked and solved in the best possible way in the years to come.

Radioactive Products of Nuclear Explosions

When a fissionable nucleus such as uranium-235 or plutonium-239 undergoes fission it produces smaller nuclei, usually two but sometimes three, as products of the fission. For example, about 3 percent by weight of the fissioned material of the bomb appears as krypton-90, a radioactive isotope of the noble gas krypton. The krypton-90 has a

43

half-life of only 25 seconds. It emits a beta ray and changes to rubidium-90, which immediately emits another beta ray and changes to strontium-90. Strontium-90 thus appears as a radioactive fission product in amount by weight about 3 percent of the fissioned material.

The total weight of the radioactive materials formed by fission is very nearly equal to the weight of the material that has undergone fission. Hydrogen bombs (fission-fusion bombs) and superbombs (fission-fusion-fission bombs) produce radioactive materials as fission products from the fission fraction of the explosive material. The fusion fraction of the explosion produces few radioactive nuclei as a direct result of fusion.

There is, however, a secondary source of radioactive material from all nuclear explosions. Large numbers of neutrons are produced by both fission and fusion. The neutrons may react with nuclei of atoms in the air, in the materials of the bomb itself, and, in case that the fireball touches the ground, in the soil and other materials of the surface of the earth, to produce new radioactive nuclei. For example, the nuclei of iron and other metals in the bomb may be made radioactive by reaction with neutrons. Large amounts of the radioactive nucleus manganese-54 have been found in ocean organisms in the Pacific. Manganese-54 is not an important product of fission, and its presence is attributed to the induced radioactivity resulting from action of neutrons on the iron-54 in the materials in the bomb or the environment. Iron-54 constitutes 5.9 percent of natural iron.

In his testimony before the Congressional hearings on fallout Dr. W. W. Kellogg of the Rand Corporation and Mr. Charles Shafer of the Radiological Defense Operations Office of the Federal Civil Defense Administration discussed the results of some thorough studies of a hypothetical attack on the United States in which nuclear bombs would be used. They said that the weapons were considered to be of three sizes, with 5-megaton, 10-megaton, and 20-megaton yields.

Let us consider what the radioactivity of the products of explosion of a 20-megaton bomb would be. We may assume it to be a fission-fusion-fission bomb, with about half fusion and half fission, so that the radioactivity would correspond to 10 megatons equivalent of fission.

The initial gamma radiation and the neutron radiation from the detonation of the bomb would kill 50 percent of all people within two and one-half miles from the point where the bomb is exploded, even though they were shielded by as much as two feet of concrete. The initial radiation is the radiation delivered within the first minute after the bomb is detonated.

The radioactivity of the fission products falls off very rapidly with time, because many of the initial fission products have very small half-lives.

After one hour the activity would be three million megacuries, and after one day it would have dropped to sixty-five thousand megacuries. A megacurie corresponds to about a ton of radium.

Much of the radioactive material in the course of time falls to the surface of the earth. This material constitutes the *radioactive fallout.*

Some of the radioactive material becomes attached to particles of moderate size, which are formed after the fireball of the exploding bomb has expanded and cooled enough to permit condensation of materials. These particles of moderate size may fall to the earth soon, within a few hours. These constitute the *local fallout.*

45

The local fallout contains only a small fraction of the radioactivity unless the fireball of the bomb touches the surface or some special materials have been added to the bomb. If the fireball touches the surface of the earth a large amount of material from the earth may be drawn up into it, to condense later into larger particles, which may incorporate the major part of the radioactivity within themselves. Dr. W. F. Libby has estimated that in this case the local fallout may contain as much as 80 percent of the fission products of a bomb.

The rest of the fission products are blown over the world by the winds of the troposphere (the lower atmosphere) and the stratosphere (the upper atmosphere, above about 7 miles, where there is no condensation of moisture in the clouds). Small bombs, in the kiloton range, spread much of their activity into the troposphere, whereas large bombs, megaton bombs, have fireballs so large that a major part of their activity, aside from that deposited in the local fallout, enters the stratosphere.

The radioactivity in the troposphere is blown about, and within a period of a few weeks is largely brought to the surface of the earth through the precipitation of rain and snow. Much of the tropospheric fallout comes to the surface of the ground in the general latitude of the site of the bomb explosion.

The radioactive materials in the stratosphere fall to ground very slowly; about 50 percent may remain in the stratosphere after 15 years. The winds in the stratosphere have time to distribute these radioactive materials nearly uniformly over the surface of the earth. During these years most of the radioactive nuclei with small half-lives decompose. Those with large half-lives in large part remain undecomposed, and retain their activity when they reach the surface of the earth, even after 20 years or more. The most important of these isotopes are strontium-90, with half-life of 28 years, and cesium-137, with half-life of 27 years.

Let us ask what might happen as a result of local fallout from a superbomb with 10 megatons equivalent of fission, the one that we have been discussing. We assume that it is exploded rather close to the earth (within a few thousand feet), and that 80 percent of the radioactivity comes to earth within an hour as local fallout.

The distribution of the local fallout will depend upon the way in which the winds close to the surface of the earth are blowing, and of course there will be more radioactivity nearby than farther away.

In order to get a rough idea of what the local fallout means, let us assume that it is spread uniformly over a circle one hundred miles in diameter (8000 square miles area), so that there is a total fallout of one megaton of fission products per thousand square miles.

From the information given by Dr. Alvin C. Graves, Science Director of the Pacific Proving Ground activities and Test Director of the Nevada Proving Ground activities of the Atomic Energy Commission, at the Congressional hearings on fallout in 1957 (*The Nature of Radioactive Fallout and Its Effects on Man,* pages 58 and 59) and that given by Dr. Ralph E. Lapp (page 1281), we can calculate what the exposure to radiation of people in this area would be.

It is found from this calculation that the total average amount of radiation at a height three feet above the surface of the ground due to the penetrating gamma rays from the fallout radioactivity would be 5500 roentgens, from one hour to one year. Of this total, 3000 roentgens would be received during the first day and 1100 roentgens from the end of the first day to the end of the first week.

This is the dosage to which unprotected persons would be exposed. Its significance is indicated by the fact that exposure to 600 roentgens during a period of a few days usually leads to death from acute radiation sickness. A large fraction of the population in this area would receive a 600-roentgen exposure within the first day or the first week after the explosion. Much of the radiation will penetrate a foot of concrete, so that protection against it is not easy.

These superbombs truly are great weapons. Superbombs of this sort have already been tested by the great nuclear powers.

If one of them were to be exploded over a large city, such as New York, the blast, fire, and immediate radiation effects would kill most of the people in the city. But even if it were to miss its target by as much as 50 miles the local fallout might descend upon the city and bring death from radiation to most of the people in the city.

Moreover, there is a possibility that still more than 80 percent of the radioactivity released in the explosion might be entrapped in such a way as to come to earth in the local fallout. Experiments have been under way on additives to these weapons such as to decrease the fraction of the radioactive products that escapes as worldwide fallout. There is a real possibility that superbombs can be made such that when exploded near the surface of the earth as much as 90 or 95 percent of the radioactive materials would come down as local fallout.

From the standpoint of the commanders of armed forces fighting a war, these weapons are ideal. There would be a maximum amount of damage done to the enemy, and a minimum amount of damage done to the people of other countries, including the homeland.

4
Radiation and Heredity

We may well stand amazed as we contemplate the nature of life, and especially of the living organism of greatest interest to us, the human being. Everything in the world is wonderful—the mountains, the ocean, the moon, the stars, crystals with their beautiful plane faces, the water that falls from the sky as rain or snow and makes streams and rivers and lakes. But living organisms—plants, animals, human beings—have something special about them.

I am glad that, while my own life is not yet ended, some insight is being obtained into the nature of living organisms, how they are made up out of atoms and molecules, and what the processes are that constitute life.

Most wonderful of all is the process of heredity. How is it possible that a man and a woman can have a child, a child whose nature is determined by theirs?

The nature of the child is determined by a small amount of material that his parents pass on to him. Since the time of Gregor Mendel and of Thomas Hunt Morgan, and through their efforts and those of many other scientists, we have come to understand in considerable detail what is involved in this process.

Every human being has inherited some genes from his father and his mother. It is estimated that he has inherited somewhere between 20,000 and 100,000 genes, half from his father and half from his mother. I think that the larger number may be a better guess than the smaller number, and I shall talk about the 100,000 genes that determine his nature.

Each of these genes is thought to be a molecule or a part of a molecule of a substance called deoxyribose nucleic acid. These are large molecules, each made up of thousands of atoms arranged in a special way, so as to constitute a sort of code. Many genes, some hundreds or thousands, are grouped together into a structure called a chromosome. For some time it was thought that human beings had 48 chromosomes; now it is thought they have only 46, and that the earlier counting (very difficult because the chromosomes are so small) was erroneous.

The nature of the child is, then, determined by the structure of the 50,000 genes that he has got from his father, in the sperm, and the 50,000 genes that he has got from his mother, in the ovum. These 100,000 molecules are very important to him, very important to the human race.

They are also extremely small; they constitute so small an amount of matter that it cannot be seen. There are in the world today about 2,700,000,000 people—nearly three billion people. They are the human race. These nearly three billion people are what they are because of the genes, 100,000 each, that they inherited from their parents. If all of these genes, 100,000 each for nearly three billion people, were to be collected together, they would form a little sphere about $\frac{1}{25}$ of an inch in diameter. This is the pool of human germ plasm that has determined the nature of the human race as it is today.

There is a similar pool of germ plasm for animals of every species, and for plants.

Mutation and Evolution

The human race, the animals, and the plants in the world have not always been here—there have been many changes.

These changes were sudden changes. It is known that a child may have a character that he did not inherit from either his father or his mother—he may have a gene that is different from the genes of his father and mother. For example, he may have a defective gene such that his blood does not clot properly, whereas his father and his mother had good genes, able to handle the job of causing clotting of the blood when necessary. One of the good genes of his parents has been changed into a bad gene, the gene for hemophilia. If he has offspring, he may pass on to his son the bad gene for hemophilia, which began, in his line of descent, with him.

The change of this good gene into the bad gene is called *mutation*.

A great deal is known about mutations. The geneticists, who study these matters, have been working very hard during the last fifty years, and they have learned many astounding things about genes and mutations and heredity.

It is known, for example, that of every 40,000 male children born, one, on the average, has a newly mutated gene for hemophilia. Something happened to this one of the 100,000 genes that he was inheriting from his parents, such as to change it from a good gene into a bad gene.

Another example is the disease achondroplasia, which is an interference with the growth of bone cartilage such as to result in dwarfism. One child in 12,500 who is born has achondroplasia because he has a new bad gene.

51

Some of the genes in the pool of human germ plasm may be much more stable than the genes that mutate into the genes for hemophilia and for achondroplasia. It is not unlikely, however, that some one of the 100,000 genes that determine the nature of a particular child is a newly mutated gene. If the average mutation rate for genes were one per 500,000 and if human beings do in fact have 100,000 genes, then it would be expected that on the average one child out of five would have one new mutant gene.

Very thorough studies have been made of mutations in fruit flies (*Drosophila*), the red bread mold (*Neurospora*), and several other species of animals and plants, and many observations have been made of mutants in man.

In all of these organisms it is found that mutations are in general deleterious, rather than beneficial. Geneticists say that only one mutation in one thousand or ten thousand or more can be expected to be beneficial, all of the others being more or less harmful.

We can understand why this is so. During the period of perhaps two billion years that has gone by since life originated on earth the genes have been improving. Now they have become almost as good as possible.

Let us consider a time in the development of the human race—a very early time—when a gene was only half as good as it might have been. Something might happen to the molecule that constituted the gene, such as to change it, to make it into a new gene. We have assumed that the gene is about half as good as it might have been; hence we may expect that the change, a random change, would have about the same chance of making it poorer as of making it better.

If the gene were made poorer the individual organism

would be less able to live and have progeny—this is what we mean by making the gene poorer. Consequently the mutant variety of the organism would die out, and the old variety would continue.

But if the gene were made better the mutant variety would be better able to live and to have progeny, and in the course of time it would have more descendants than the unmutated individuals. Then the new variety, resulting from the mutation, would have taken over. This is the process of evolution through mutation and natural selection.

A long operation of this process, with the better and better mutant genes replacing the poorer genes in the pool of germ plasm, can be expected to have resulted in a pool of human germ plasm consisting of genes that are nearly as good as possible. This is the situation at the present time. Every species of plant or animal is determined by a pool of germ plasm that has been most carefully selected over a period of hundreds of millions of years.

We can understand now why it is that mutations in these carefully selected organisms almost invariably are detrimental. The situation can be suggested by a statement made by Dr. J. B. S. Haldane: My clock is not keeping perfect time. It is conceivable that it will run better if I shoot a bullet through it; but it is much more probable that it will stop altogether. Professor George Beadle, in this connection, has asked: "What is the chance that a typographical error would improve Hamlet?"

There is still the possibility of a genetic improvement in human beings. The world of today is different from that of a few hundred or a few thousand years ago. Some

53

of the characters that were the best for life in the world as it was some time ago may not be the best now. Possibly some natural mutations will occur that will improve the human race, if some humane way of permitting the mutant variety to increase can be devised. Natural selection is a cruel way, and man has now outgrown it. The problem is not to be solved by increasing the mutation rate, and thus increasing the number of defective children born, but rather by finding some acceptable replacement for natural selection.

It is true that extraordinary advances have been made in plant and animal breeding. The reason for this is simple. In a breeding program a great many mutants may be produced (by the use of x-radiation, as described below). Almost all of them are harmful, but these mutant individuals are eliminated from the line. The mutant with the rare beneficial mutation—that is, beneficial by man's standard, though probably rarely, if ever, to the organism itself —is recognized by the person who is carrying on the breeding program, and a new variety of plant or animal is then obtained by breeding this mutant.

This is a special sort of selection—with man taking a hand in it.

Man is also taking a hand in the process of natural selection in human beings, but not in such a way as to improve the pool of human germ plasm. In earlier times the physically and mentally handicapped individual human beings were weeded out; they were not able to compete with their more fortunate brethren in having children. But with the development of modern man, with his strong feelings about humanity, the process is working the other way. In the modern world there is a greater and greater tendency for the handicapped individuals to be nurtured. As a result of this and also of medical progress, there is now a less effective process of weeding the bad genes out of the pool of human germ plasm than was operating even a few centuries ago.

There are many bad genes in the pool of human germ plasm. The number of bad genes is determined by the rate at which new ones are being formed and the rate at which they are being removed from the pool. A steady state has been set up, with these two rates equal to each other.

The rate at which the bad genes are being formed through mutation has been discussed above for hemophilia and achondroplasia. If some of the bad genes for these diseases were not removed from the pool of human germ plasm, the number of children born with these diseases would increase with every generation, because of the new mutations. In fact, children who are born with hemophilia do not in general have offspring—the number of their offspring is only one-eighth of that for normal individuals. Consequently, most of the genes for hemophilia are not passed on to the next generation. This is the way in which the steady state is set up.

If something were to happen in the world that doubled the mutation rate for all genes, a new steady state would be set up in which the number of bad genes in the pool of human germ plasm would be twice as great as at the present time. Then there would be twice as many children born with hemophilia, twice as many with achondroplasia, twice as many defective in other ways determined by these bad genes.

If there were to be a great war fought with nuclear weapons the mutation rate for human beings might be doubled, might be tripled, might become ten times as great. There is even the possibility that such a war might

not leave enough human beings alive for following generations to arise, or might cause such great changes in the
pool of human germ plasm that the following generations
would hardly be recognized as human beings.

Even the bomb tests are having an effect in increasing
the mutation rate and consequently increasing the amount
of human suffering.

Radiation and Mutation

Until about thirty years ago nobody in the world knew
what causes genes to mutate. In 1927 Dr. H. J. Muller,
who was then in the University of Texas and is now
Professor of Genetics in Indiana University, discovered
that exposure of plants and animals to x-rays causes an
increase in the number of mutations.

This was a great discovery, for which Dr. Muller was
given the Nobel Prize in 1946. His discovery has made it
possible for breeders of plants and animals to improve the
strains more rapidly than was possible before, because by
use of x-rays larger numbers of mutants can be produced
and the favorable ones selected, the unfavorable ones
rejected and not allowed to have progeny.

Perhaps even more important for man is that Dr.
Muller's discovery has made it possible for the geneticist
to make more penetrating and more extensive studies of
the processes of inheritance and mutation than in the old
days, when they had to work with only the small number
of mutants that are produced naturally.

All kinds of high-energy radiation produce mutations.
Cosmic rays, gamma rays, beta rays, and alpha rays are
all effective if they reach the reproductive organs.

The number of mutations produced by various ionizing radiations is very nearly proportional to the ionizing power of the radiations, measured in roentgens. Accordingly we may discuss the action of the cosmic rays, natural radioactivity, and fallout radioactivity in producing mutations in terms of the exposure of the reproductive organs as measured in roentgens.

The number of new mutant genes that a child has is determined in part by the amount of radiation to which the reproductive organs of the parent have been exposed before the child was conceived. The average age of parents at the conception of children is thirty years, and accordingly the effects of radiation on future generations are determined by the average amount of exposure to radiation of the reproductive organs (the gonads—that is, the ovaries and testes) of the parents before they have reached the age of thirty years. The amount of background radiation—from cosmic rays and natural radioactivity—to which the gonads of human beings are exposed during the first thirty years of life depends somewhat upon the environment of the human being (altitude, nature of the rock or soil in the region, amount of radium in the drinking water, etc.). Estimates of the amount have been discussed in the preceding chapter. A reasonable estimate is 0.110 roentgens per year, which corresponds to 3.3 roentgens in thirty years.

Nobody knows how many mutations in human beings are caused by this background radiation.

Geneticists believe that mutations are produced in human beings by radiation, even the small amount of radiation that constitutes the background of cosmic rays and natural radioactivity. Geneticists also believe that the number of mutations in human beings caused by radia-

57

tion is proportional to the amount of radiation that reaches the gonads.

The direct evidence for this belief is not very great. Experiments cannot be carried out with human beings, as they are with other organisms. There is some direct evidence of production of mutations in human beings by rather small amounts of x-radiation. Dr. James F. Crow, Professor of Genetics and Zoology at the University of Wisconsin, made a questionnaire study showing that a somewhat larger number of abnormal births have occurred in the families of American radiologists, who are exposed to x-rays in the course of their work, than in a group of physicians who did not use x-rays in their work. A somewhat similar study made in France by Dr. J. LeJeune and coworkers showed an apparent effect on the children of parents who had received x-ray treatments for various diseases.

The strongest evidence about the production of mutations in man by radiation is that obtained by experiments on other animals. Scores of species of animals and plants have been thoroughly tested, and every one of them has been found to have in increase in mutation rate upon exposure to ionizing radiation. As Dr. Curt Stern, a distinguished geneticist in the University of California in Berkeley, has said, "Who is there who believes that man is different, in this respect, from all the other organisms that have been investigated—animals, plants, bacteria, protozoa, in every one of which mutations are produced by x-rays?"

Even with plants and experimental animals, it has been difficult to obtain experimental proof that an amount of radiation as small as the background radiation produces mutations. However, the experiments have been carried out (by Professors Warren P. Spencer and Curt Stern) with exposures as small as 25 roentgens and 50 roentgens, and the number of additional mutations has been found to be proportional to the amount of exposure, to within the experimental error of the studies. Moreover, it makes no difference whether the gonads are exposed to a single large dose of radiation or to many very small ones spread over a long period of time—the number of mutations is determined by the total exposure.

These are the reasons that geneticists believe that radiation produces mutations in man, and that even the small additional amount of radiation that comes from fallout radioactivity is producing mutations, proportional in number to the amount of the fallout. These are the reasons that the distinguished scientists of the Committee on Genetic Effects of Atomic Radiation of the U.S. National Research Council-National Academy of Sciences said in their report that *"Any radiation is genetically undesirable,* since any radiation induces harmful mutations. Further, all presently available scientific information leads to the conclusion that *the genetic harm is proportional to the total dose* (that is, the total accumulated dose to the reproductive cells from the conception of the parents to the conception of the child)." In their recommendations they said "As geneticists we say: *keep the dose as low as you can,"* and that "the basic fact is—and no competent persons doubt this—that radiations produce mutations and that mutations are in general harmful. It is difficult at the present state of knowledge of genetics to estimate just how much of what kind of harm will appear in each future generation, after mutant genes are induced by radiations. Different geneticists prefer differing ways of describing this situation: But they all come out with the unanimous conclusion that the potential danger is raised."

Part of the danger to future generations is that of damage to the pool of human germ plasm by exposure of the gonads to medical x-rays, used for diagnostic and therapeutic purposes, and also to radiation exposure of workers in industry and of human beings generally to artificial radioactivity produced in nuclear power plants.

These problems are serious problems. The National Academy of Sciences-National Research Council Committee estimated that the average exposure of the gonads of people in America to medical x-rays is at the present time about as great as the exposure to background radiation. If this were to continue, there would result a considerable increase, perhaps as great as ten or twenty percent, in the number of defective children born in future generations. There has been much concern about this problem, especially since the publication of the report of the Committee of the National Academy of Sciences-National Research Council.

Vigorous efforts are now being taken to decrease the amount of exposure of the gonads of young people to medical x-radiation and to radiation from other sources. For example, the Surgeon General of the United States in November 1957 issued a strong recommendation that there be in the future no mass programs of x-radiography or fluoroscopy as a method of finding tuberculosis, except among high-risk groups, and that x-ray examination be in general restricted to persons giving a positive reaction to tuberculin skin tests. Even with chest x-rays or dental x-rays a fraction of the x-radiation is scattered to the gonads.

In the efforts to decrease the genetic damage to the pool of human germ plasm that is done by medical x-rays we must always balance the damage that is done by the radia-

tion against the benefit that can come from the early discovery of a pathological condition or from the treatment
of the cancer or other disease by x-ray methods. When this
balance is made, I think that it will turn out that the
amount of gonadal exposure to medical x-rays can be kept
to one tenth of the present amount, perhaps even to one
twentieth. One step in this direction that is now being
taken is the introduction of x-ray photographic films that
permit the exposure time to be reduced by 25 percent.
Further progress in both radiography and fluoroscopy may
be expected in the future, and an additional decrease in
the amount of exposure may result also from progress
in the methods of medical practice.

In every aspect of modern life that involves radiation
we must remember the admonition of the NAS-NRC Committee: *keep the dose as low as you can.*

Gonadal Exposure from Fallout Radioactivity

The tests of nuclear weapons that have been carried out
by the United States, the U.S.S.R., and Great Britain are
producing mutations of the genes in human beings, such
that there will be an increase in the number of defective
children born in later generations.

If we want to estimate how many defective children will
be caused to be born by the fallout radioactivity, we must
first make an estimate of the amount of added exposure to
radiation that the gonads of human beings are subjected
to as a result of the fallout.

This quantity cannot be estimated with great precision.
It is likely that it is about 10 percent of the exposure due
to background radiation.

A large part of the exposure of the gonads to fallout

61

radiation is that to the gamma radiation coming from radioactive materials that have fallen to the surface of the earth. Some additional exposure is from the gamma radiation of cesium-137 that has been taken into the human body.

One source of radiation to the gonads and other parts of the body that has received little attention is carbon-14 from fallout. There is a total amount of about 160,000 pounds of natural carbon-14 in the atmosphere, biosphere, and ocean. It is made by cosmic rays from nitrogen nuclei.

Dr. Willard F. Libby, Atomic Energy Commissioner, in his address of 27 March 1958 before the symposium on fallout arranged by the Swiss Academy of Medical Sciences, reported an estimate of the amount of carbon-14 released by bomb tests. For 10 megatons of bombs (both fission and fusion, in the customary ratio), about 160 pounds of carbon-14 is made. The increase of the concentration of carbon-14 in the atmosphere so far has been by about 10 percent, because of the tests.

Dr. Libby has stated that "The total gamma dose rate from fallout in the inhabited regions of the Northern Hemisphere at the present time is of the order of one to five milliroentgens per year." This corresponds to from 0.03 to 0.15 roentgens in thirty years.

From information provided by the Atomic Energy Commission, the Committee on Genetic Effects of Atomic Radiation of the National Academy of Sciences-National Research Council in 1956 reported, after a brief discussion of the factors involved, that "With these understandings it may be stated that U.S. residents have, on the average, been receiving from fallout over the past five years a dose which, if weapons testing were continued at the present rate, is estimated to produce a total 30-year dose of about *one-tenth of a roentgen,* and since the accuracy involved is not better than a factor of five, one could better say that the 30-year dose from weapons testing if maintained at the past level would probably be larger than 0.02 roentgens and smaller than 0.50 roentgens."

It is not clear whether or not the effect of cesium-137 ingested into the human body has been taken into consideration in these estimates; it is only recently that the hazard of cesium-137 has been recognized. In a discussion of information obtained by Japanese scientists, Professor Iwao Ogawa of the St. Paul's University in Tokyo reported in the January 1958 issue of the *Bulletin of the Atomic Scientists* that the amount of cesium-137 found in foodstuffs in Japan corresponds to internal irradiation of the gonads by gamma rays of 0.070 roentgens in 30 years, which is to be added to the external gamma radiation.

The estimate of the 30-year gonad dose of fallout radiation made by Dr. Ralph E. Lapp and Dr. Jack Schubert in their book *Radiation: What It Is and How It Affects You* (page 195) is 0.5 roentgen in 30 years for people living in the United States. These two scientists have devoted great effort to the interpretation and analysis of all available information about fallout. It was Dr. Lapp who, making use of his scientific knowledge and reasoning powers, reached the conclusion (independently reached also by Dr. Joseph Rotblat, of St. Bartholomew's Hospital, London) that the 1 March 1954 bomb was a bomb of a new kind, involving a third fission stage of uranium-238, long before the Atomic Energy Commission released this information.

The fallout exposure of people in the Southern Hemisphere is somewhat less than that of people in the Northern Hemisphere. However, the difference is not a great one and there are not many people living in the Southern Hemisphere, so that the correction to be applied to the estimates for the United States in order to make them applicable to the whole world is not large, not more than 10 percent.

I have made the estimate that bomb testing at the present rate gives an average radiation exposure to the gonads of people in the world of 0.3 roentgen. This is somewhat less than the estimate made by Dr. Lapp and Dr. Schubert, roughly midway between the extreme values given by the Committee of the NAS-NRC, and somewhat larger than the probable value quoted by this Committee.

An official statement by the Atomic Energy Commission (Report by the United States Atomic Energy Commission on the Effects of High-Yield Nuclear Explosions, page 1954 of *The Nature of Radioactive Fallout and Its Effects on Man*) contains the following statement:

"In general, the total amount of radiation received by residents of the United States from all nuclear detonations to date, including the Russian and British tests and all of our own tests in the United States and the Pacific, has been about one-tenth of a roentgen." This sentence is in the section of the report dealing with the genetic effects of radiation, and the quantity mentioned presumably is the exposure of the gonads. Inasmuch as the bomb tests that had been carried out up to the time of the report, February 1955, amounted to only about 50 megatons of fission, this value corresponds to an estimate of about 0.6 roentgen exposure of the gonads during a period of 30 years for testing at the present rate. This estimate is probably less reliable than the later estimate 0.1 roentgen in 30 years.

I do not know about any recent authoritative discussion

of the important question of the average gonad exposure from bomb testing at the present rate. A rough calculation may have some value. If we assume that fallout reaches the ground in an average time of one month (Dr. Libby gives two weeks to one month for tropospheric fallout, and several years, perhaps ten years, for stratospheric fallout) and that it is uniformly distributed over the surface of the earth, we calculate from information given in *The Nature of Radioactive Fallout and Its Effects on Man,* (pages 58 and 1281) that gonad exposure for an unprotected person would be 1.9 roentgens in 30 years, at the present rate of testing (10 megatons of fission per year). This value should be increased somewhat, perhaps by 50 percent, because most of the tropospheric fallout occurs in the Northern Hemisphere, where most of the people of the world live. It should be decreased somewhat, perhaps by dividing by 10, because some of the radioactivity is washed away or penetrates deep into the soil and because people are protected to some extent by living in houses. (In Japan, where most people live in wooden houses, the estimated correction factor is about ⅓, in the United States about ⅒, and in Great Britain about 1/20.) With this correction we get 0.3 roentgens in 30 years for gonad exposure from external radiation, to which should be added that from internal radiation (ingested cesium-137).

This calculation is unreliable, because it is based on bits of published information. A detailed and thoroughly documented discussion by AEC authorities would be welcomed by all scientists interested in this question. Even as late as January 1958, when the 23rd Semiannual Report of the U.S. Atomic Energy Commission was published, the value used in discussing genetic effects (page 460) was the old one of 1956: "It is estimated in the NAS report that in the United States the accumulated 30-year dose will be about 0.1 roentgen, if weapons testing continues at the average rate of the previous five years." But in the NAS-NRC report this estimate is attributed to the AEC and the Armed Forces, and no details about how it was made have been published. Surely during the two years that have now gone by much more information has been gathered. We should now be told whether the present estimate is the same, or is the five times higher value mentioned in the NAS-NRC report as a possibility, or perhaps a lower value.

I think that my estimate of 0.3 roentgen in 30 years as the average gonad exposure for bomb testing at the present rate is a reasonable one to use in the discussion of the genetic effects of fallout radioactivity at the present time. It lies close to the average of the estimates that have been made.

I believe that it is the average that should be used, for the following reason. Let us assume two possible extreme values, which have equal probability, such as 0.02 roentgen in 30 years and 0.6 roentgen in 30 years, the smallest and the largest of the values given above. If 0.1 roentgen in 30 years gives an increase in mutation rate that will lead in the course of time to the birth of, say, 10,000 seriously defective children, then 0.02 roentgen would lead to 2000 and 0.6 roentgen to 60,000. If these extremes have equal probability the average expectation value is 31,000 defective children. This average would also be given by using the average of the two values of the radiation exposure. Accordingly, I believe that it is justified to use an average value of the estimated amounts of exposure, and I have selected 0.3 roentgen in 30 years as this average.

This value of the gonad exposure due to fallout radio-activity is about 10 percent of the background exposure of the gonads, and it would accordingly be expected to cause an increase in mutation rate equal to about 10 percent of the mutation rate due to the background radiation.

Fallout and Defective Children

Every year about 75,000,000 children are born in the world. About 2 percent of the children that are born have obvious serious defects that are due to heredity, to bad genes. Thus about 1,500,000 children with serious hereditary defects are born in the world each year. Many more suffer from less serious hereditary defects.

Nobody knows just how many of these defective children are the result of bad genes that have been caused by background radiation. Some geneticists think that as many as 50 percent of the mutations are due to background radiation, and others think that only about 2 percent are due to background radiation. The average amount estimated by geneticists is about 10 percent. The geneticist H. J. Muller, who discovered that x-rays produce mutations, has given 6 percent as his estimate.

I shall make use of the estimate that 10 percent of the mutations in man at the present time have been produced by background radiation.

With the value 0.3 roentgen in 30 years as the exposure of the gonads to fallout radioactivity, which is 10 percent of the background radiation, we are then led to the conclusion that an estimated value of the effect of testing of nuclear weapons at the present rate is an increase by 1 percent in the mutation rate.

This conclusion that bomb testing at the present rate

leads to about 1 percent increase in mutation agrees with the estimates of several authorities in the field of genetics. For example, Dr. George W. Beadle, the distinguished geneticist who is Chairman of the Biology Division of the California Institute of Technology, has authorized me to say that in his public statements he makes use of his own estimate of 1 percent increase in mutation rate as a result of bomb testing at the present rate. Dr. Sewall Wright, Professor of Genetics in the University of Wisconsin, has written me that his estimate also is 1 percent.

The recent estimate given by the AEC Advisory Committee on Biology and Medicine (October 1957; published in the 23rd Semiannual Report of the AEC, 1958, page 410) is 0.2 percent to 1 percent increase in mutation rate and ultimate increase in genetically defective children. I think that the larger value, 1 percent, is the more likely one, but our following arguments would be changed by use of the smaller value, 0.2 percent, only in that the estimated numbers would be somewhat smaller; the moral problem would remain the same.

An increase in the mutation rate means that more bad genes are placed in the pool of human germ plasm, more seriously defective children are born. Almost all of the mutant genes are bad ones—extremely few are beneficial. A 1-percent increase in the number of bad genes means tragedy for many human beings.

The genetic effect of the bomb tests can be described in either of two ways. One may say that the increase is a very small one, perhaps that it is negligible. One may say that the deleterious genetic effects of fallout radioactivity are less than the deleterious genetic effects of cosmic rays and natural radioactivity, that the risk that one runs of having a defective child may be increased more by one's moving from sea level to the altitude of Denver, or by moving from a wood house to a stone house, than it has been increased by the bomb tests. One may say that a person who wears a wrist watch with a rather strongly radioactive dial incurs in consequence of this a greater chance of having a defective child than he incurs because radiation from fallout radioactivity is passing through him as a result of the bomb tests. One may say that the exposure of the testes of a commercial airplane pilot to the radiation from the radioactive dials of the instruments on his instrument panel causes him to incur a greater chance of having a defective child than the fallout radioactivity does. One may say that the increase in the number of defective children as a result of the bomb tests is undetectable—this is true, because medical statistics are not good enough at the present time to detect an increase by 1 percent in the number of defective children born.

In fact, all of the above statements are true, and all of them have been made by spokesmen for the Atomic Energy Commission.

I think, however, that they do not tell the whole story. I believe that one goal that human beings strive for is that of decreasing the amount of human suffering in the world, and that it is worth while to ask how many individual defective children will be born in the world as a result of the testing of nuclear weapons.

How many seriously defective children are caused by the bomb tests?

Dr. James F. Crow gave testimony about his estimate of the effect of fallout radioactivity on children born in future generations before the Special Congressional Subcommittee on Radiation (*The Nature of Radioactive Fallout and Its Effects on Man*, page 1021). He made his estimate for a gonad exposure of 0.1 roentgen during a 30-year period. In the table below the second column gives his estimate of defects or deaths of the sorts mentioned during the first generation, and the third column gives the total for all future generations. I have put in the fourth column the estimate for one year of testing at the rate 0.1 roentgen in 30 years, and in the last column the estimate for one year of testing at the rate 0.3 roentgen in 30 years, which is my estimate of fallout radioactivity.

We may use another way of making an estimate of the genetic effect of fallout radioactivity. Each year 1,500,000 seriously defective children are born in the world because they have had the bad luck to have some defective genes among the set of 100,000 that they have received from the pool of human germ plasm. One child in about one thousand has the disease cystic fibrosis of the pancreas, caused by bad genes; he is seriously affected and usually dies within a few years. The bad genes that cause diabetes, hemophilia, muscular dystrophy, microcephaly (incomplete development of the brain), achondroplasia, and many other diseases are increased by the fallout radioactivity. One out of one hundred of the mentally deficient patients in the mental hospitals in the United States has inherited the bad genes for the disease phenylketonuria; it is these genes that cause his mental deficiency. Probably more than one half of all the mentally deficient individuals in the world have their mental defect because of bad genes. Professor L. S. Penrose of the University of London has estimated that one child in two hundred who is born will become schizophrenic because of his inheritance of a gene for schizophrenia, and that one in two hundred who is born will have manic depressive attacks because of bad genes.

To the child himself who is born to a life of suffering

Table 2

Estimated Effect of Bomb Tests on Future Generations
(After Professor James F. Crow)

Kind of damage*	Number in 1st generation (0.1 roentgen in 30 years)	Total for future generations (0.1 roentgen in 30 years)	Total for future generations per year of testing at 0.1 roentgen in 30 years	Total for future generations per year of testing at 0.3 roentgen in 30 years
Gross physical or mental defect	8,000	80,000	2,700	8,000
Stillbirths and childhood deaths	20,000	300,000	10,000	30,000
Embryonic and neonatal deaths	40,000	700,000	23,000	70,000

*Note: Plus a larger but unknown number of minor or intangible defects.

or early death and to his parents the inheritance of the mutant genes is a tragedy.

According to my estimate, the bomb tests at the present rate will, in the course of time, lead to an increase of 1 percent in the number of defective births—this corresponds to the 1 percent increase in the mutation rate. When this steady state has been set up, in case that testing is continued at the present rate of 10 megatons of fission per year, there will be born each year in the world about 15,000 seriously defective children (1 percent of 1,500,000), seriously defective children whose defect is to be attributed to the bomb tests.

This number does not include embryonic and neonatal deaths and stillbirths. It is to be compared with the number 8000 children with gross physical and mental defects plus a part of the 30,000 stillbirths and childhood deaths (the part corresponding to childhood deaths) given in the last column of the table representing Dr. Crow's estimates. The two estimates are seen to agree in order of magnitude.

If the bomb tests are continued, it will be some generations before the genetic steady state is closely approached. The effects of the present bomb tests will appear in the first generation of progeny, and also in the second generation and many future generations, not dying out, even if the bomb tests were to be stopped now, until after forty or fifty generations have gone by.

The steady-state number of seriously defective children, 15,000 per year, is just the number that can be attributed to the mutations caused by the bomb tests of a single year at the present rate. We may say that each year of bomb testing at the present rate is carried out with the sacrifice of 15,000 children, who would be born healthy and would lead normal lives if the bomb tests had not been carried out that year, but who, because of those bomb tests, will be born with serious physical or mental defects.

The great superbomb that was tested by the United States on 1 March 1954 released radioactivity roughly equal to that of one year of testing at the present rate. We may hence say that the testing of one great superbomb, with 10 megatons of fission, requires the sacrifice of 15,000 children.

I believe that the national leader who gives the order to test the nuclear weapon and to release the fission products corresponding to 10 megatons of fission should know that in giving this order he is dooming 15,000 unborn children to a life of misery or early death.

Perhaps the estimate that bomb testing at the present rate is producing a 1 percent increase in mutation rate is wrong. There is a possibility that it is ten times too large. Also there is a possibility (because our knowledge is incomplete) that it is ten times too small. Perhaps the testing of one large superbomb requires the sacrifice of only 1500 children, perhaps it requires the sacrifice of 150,000 children, or even more.

The Menace of Carbon-14

We are the custodians of the human race. We have the duty of protecting the pool of human germ plasm against willful damage.

If the human race survives the present era of nuclear peril, damage will continue to be done to the pool of human germ plasm by the radioactive elements created in the nuclear test explosions that have been carried out during the past few years and present year.

The most menacing radioactive substance of all of those

73

produced in the bomb tests is carbon-14. It is a great menace because it lives so long—over 8000 years—and because it is produced in large amounts—about 16 pounds per megaton of explosive energy.

Also, there is no such thing as a clean nuclear bomb with respect to carbon-14. It is made by both fusion and fission. Some of the neutrons from every bomb—fission alone, or fission-fusion, or fission-fusion-fission—escape and combine with nitrogen nuclei of the air to form carbon-14.

The entire atmosphere, the ocean, and the biosphere (plants and animals) used to contain about 160,000 pounds of carbon-14, produced in the upper atmosphere by cosmic rays. During the past four years the amount in the atmosphere has been increased by 10 percent because of the bomb tests. If the tests are continued at the 1958 rate the amount in the atmosphere will be doubled in a few years.

Dr. Willard F. Libby has now released enough information in his address of 27 March 1958 to the Swiss Academy of Medical Sciences to permit a calculation to be made of the predicted effects of carbon-14 due to the bomb tests.

Dr. Libby has estimated 0.0015 roentgen per year as the irradiation of the gonads by natural carbon-14. An added 10 percent of bomb-test carbon-14 would produce 0.00015 roentgen per year, or 0.0045 roentgen in the genetically important first 30 years of life.

This is about one or two ten-thousandths of the amount that doubles the mutation rate. It will hence increase the number of defective children born by 0.01 or 0.02 percent, which is about 150 to 300 per year.

But the carbon-14 released in the period 1952 to 1958 will continue to act for thousands of years. I have made a calculation of the total predicted effect on the basis of the following assumptions: the rate of bomb testing (fission plus fusion) is 30 megatons per year; one third of the generated carbon-14 is released to the atmosphere; the amount generated is 16 pounds per megaton, as stated by Dr. Libby; after some years a steady state is reached between the atmosphere and the ocean, the whole reservoir having a normal content of 160,000 pounds of carbon-14; the normal amount of carbon-14 in the human body produces a gonad exposure of 0.0015 roentgen per year, as stated in 1956 by Dr. Libby; the genetic effects of gonad radiation are as estimated by Dr. Crow and given in Table 2; the mean life of carbon-14 is 8070 years; the population of the world, which has increased by over 1 billion during the last 100 years, will continue to increase and will have an average value during the next 10,000 years such that there will be five times as many children born as at present.

This straightforward calculation leads directly to the conclusion that one year of testing at the standard rate of 30 megatons per year will ultimately be responsible for the birth of 230,000 seriously defective children (gross mental or physical defect or stillbirth or childhood death) and also for 420,000 embryonic and neonatal deaths.

The bomb tests carried out so far (about 150 megatons, including 1958) will ultimately produce about 1 million seriously defective children and about 2 million embryonic and neonatal deaths, and will cause many millions of people to suffer from minor hereditary defects.

Carbon-14 is a greater menace to the human race than the shorter-lived radioactive elements, whose effects were discussed earlier in this chapter. No warning about the genetic effects of carbon-14 has been issued by the AEC, and only in March 1958 was information released on which the above estimates of their magnitude could be based.

The foregoing argument is a reliable one. Geneticists

are in general agreement about every point upon which it is based.

The geneticists are sure that no one can claim that the genetic effect does not exist. We must all accept the fact that the testing of nuclear weapons is carried out at the expense of the lives of children as yet unborn.

5
Radiation and Disease

Are there hundreds of thousands of people living in the world today who will die ten or fifteen or twenty years before their normal time of death because of the tests of nuclear weapons that have been carried out?

Nobody can answer this question with certainty, at the present time. In common with many other scientists, I believe that the question is to be answered by the word "Yes." There are also some scientists with competency in the field who think that it probably should be answered "No."

There is no doubt that radiation such as that from fall-out radioactivity can cause human beings to die of leukemia, bone cancer, and other diseases.

It is known that if a thousand people were to be given doses of x-rays amounting to 1000 roentgens, about fifty of them could be expected to develop leukemia and to die of this disease during the next 25 years. Leukemia is a kind of cancer of the cells that manufacture the white corpuscles of the blood.

What would happen if each one of one million people were to receive an exposure of 1 roentgen? This is the same total amount of irradiation as 1000 people receiving 1000 roentgens each. Would it be expected that fifty of the one million people would develop leukemia during the next 25 years, or would none of them develop leukemia, as a result of the irradiation?

At the present time the genetic effects of fallout radioactivity can be discussed with confidence. All scientists agree about these effects, except for some differences in the estimates of the number of defective children that will result from a certain exposure of the gonads to fallout radioactivity. The question of the effects of fallout radioactivity in causing leukemia and other diseases in persons now living cannot be discussed with the same certainty.

I shall give some reasons for my belief, which is held also by many other scientists, that it is probable that small amounts of radiation, as well as large amounts, cause leukemia, bone cancer, and other diseases in human beings, with the probability of the incurrence of the disease proportional to the amount of radiation. I shall give the results of calculations based upon this assumption. I shall, from time to time, repeat the statement that the somatic effects of fallout radioactivity that are being discussed are uncertain in the degree that this belief is uncertain.

Acute Radiation Sickness

If the entire body of a human being is exposed to 1000 roentgens or more of gamma radiation or other ionizing radiation at one time or within a short period (one day), he begins to suffer from acute radiation sickness, and dies in a few days. For example, in the second fatal radiation accident (21 May 1946) in the Los Alamos Scientific Laboratory, where the first atomic bomb work was done, a 32-year-old man who had been working with fissionable material was accidentally exposed to about 2000 roentgens of radiation. During the first few hours he vomited several times. Then for several days his condition was good. On the fifth day the number of white cells in his blood fell rapidly, and on the sixth day his temperature and pulse rate rose. On the seventh day he had periods of mental confusion, then he gradually sank into a coma and died on the ninth day.

Another man, 34 years old, received an average dose of 415 roentgens to his body. He was somewhat nauseated the first day, his temperature rose slightly on the fifth and sixth days to 102.6°F, and he complained of drowsiness, lack of appetite, and constipation. He was given penicillin therapy, and his temperature gradually fell to normal. He was discharged on the fifteenth day, and slowly regained his normal weight and strength. His hair fell out and began to grow back only after four or five months. An examination of the sperm and testicle tissue indicated that sterility had been caused by the radiation, but after five years the sperm count returned to normal and he became the father of an apparently normal child. He developed radiation cataracts in both eyes.

The amount of full-body radiation that causes death is somewhere between 300 roentgens and 600 roentgens. The amount 450 roentgens is estimated to cause death by radiation sickness in 50 percent of the recipients.

Many of the fatalities in Hiroshima and Nagasaki were the result of radiation sickness.

Radiation sickness, though important in the discussion of nuclear warfare, has little importance for the bomb tests. Except for the few accidental deaths that have occurred in connection with the development of nuclear weapons and the possible case of one Japanese fisherman on the fishing boat *The Fortunate Dragon,* no deaths from acute radiation sickness have been reported in the nuclear weapons programs.

The Little Bullets

The effect of a large amount of radiation on the human body in causing death from acute radiation sickness is somewhat similar to the effect of a lethal dose of an ordinary poison—perhaps closer to that of a mixture of ordinary poisons.

But radiation has other effects that are different from the effect of an ordinary poison. These effects may result from even very small exposures to radiation.

A person may swallow an amount of a poison one thousandth of the lethal dose without doing himself any harm whatever. He may repeat this small dose day after day for one thousand days without harming himself; whereas if he had taken the one thousand small doses at one time he would have been killed. For example, he may take one sleeping pill each night for one thousand nights in succession without harm to himself, although he would have died if he had swallowed the thousand pills at one time.

But the properties of radiation are different. It is known that exposure of the reproductive organs of animals to 100 roentgens of radiation causes the same amount of damage to the genes, the same number of mutations, when the exposure is made in many small doses spread over a long period of time as when it is made in a single dose. It is probable also that many small doses of radiation are as effective in causing leukemia and bone cancer and some other diseases as a single large dose of an equal amount of radiation.

A very small amount of an ordinary chemical poison may do no harm whatever to a person; but a very small amount of radiation may harm him in such a way as to cause him to die or to have a seriously defective child.

We can understand this strange and terrible effect of radiation by considering the way in which radiation interacts with the molecules that compose the human body.

The rays of high-energy radiation are like little bullets that shoot through the body. They tear electrons away from molecules, and through subsequent reactions of the molecular ions that are formed the molecules may be broken in two, some atoms may be torn away from them, some new molecules may be formed.

The exposure of the human body to 1 roentgen of radiation causes about a thousand ions to be formed in each cell of the human body—one thousand new molecules, perhaps poisonous, in each cell. The dose of 500 roentgens that usually leads to death by acute radiation sickness causes about 500,000 changed molecules to be formed in each cell.

Some of the new molecules that are produced by the radiation are poisonous. If enough of them are made in the body of a human being he will die in a few days. He has died of acute radiation sickness.

In most of the cells of the human body there are, among the billions of molecules of many different kinds, a few very important ones. These are the molecules, probably molecules of deoxyribose nucleic acid, that govern the behavior of the cell, that control the manufacture of other molecules and the process by which the cell divides to form new cells, and that determine the nature of the children who are born to the person.

If one of these special molecules happens to be damaged

81

by a single little bullet of radiation from a single radioactive atom, it may be changed in such a way as to cause
the cell to divide much more rapidly than the other cells
of the body. This cell may then produce a colony of rapidly
dividing cells, which in the course of time would out-
number the normal cells of that type. Then the human
being may die from cancer—perhaps leukemia, bone cancer, some other kind of cancer—caused by the single radioactive atom that produced the single little bullet of radiation.

This is the reason why the radioactive atoms, such as
strontium-90 and cesium-137, that are being spread all
over the world by the bomb tests are harmful. *There is no
safe amount of radiation or of radioactive material. Even
small amounts do harm.*

There is no doubt that the small amounts of radiation
received by every human being from cosmic rays, natural
radioactivity, and fallout radioactivity cause gene mutations that increase the number of defective children born
in future generations. Geneticists agree on this, and their
estimates of the number of defective children caused by
a given small amount of radiation are reasonably con-
sistent.

On the other hand, there is still some doubt about the
magnitude of the somatic effect of radiation—its effect in
causing direct damage to human beings. At the present
time scientists disagree about the question of whether a
small amount of radiation, say 10 roentgens, has one tenth
the probability of causing the exposed person to contract
leukemia or bone cancer or some other disease as that of
exposure to one hundred roentgens, or whether the probability is considerably less than one tenth, or even somewhat more.

I believe, as do many other scientists, that it is highly probable that the effects of radiation in causing cancer are closely proportional to the amount of the radiation, even for small amounts, of a few roentgens in a lifetime. The estimates that are made in the following sections of this book are based upon this assumption.

Ionizing radiation in amounts of the order of hundreds of roentgens or thousands of roentgens causes cancer and other diseases. Within a year after the discovery of x-rays it was noticed that radiologists and technicians working with x-ray tubes often developed burns on the hands, forearms, and face, which in some cases developed into cancer of the skin. Cancer of the skin has also been found in many patients who received treatment with x-rays or radioactive rays from radium for mild skin infections or for the removal of facial hair.

Cancer of the thyroid gland, cancer of the pharynx, and cancer of the larynx have been reported among children some years after they were given x-ray treatment for conditions including suspected enlargement of the thymus gland, bronchitis, infected tonsils and adenoids, and enlarged glands in the neck, the exposure being in some cases as low as 250 roentgens.

Leukemia has developed with increased incidence in many populations that have received large amounts of radiation in a single dose or in a succession of small doses.

Many reports of death by cancer have been made since 1925 among the workers who during the period from 1916 to 1924 were engaged in the painting of watch and clock dials with a luminous paint containing radium or other radioactive elements (mesothorium, radiothorium). These workers applied the paint to the dials with brushes, and many of them were accustomed to bringing the brush to a fine point by putting it between their lips. In this way they swallowed radioactive materials, which were incorporated into the bones. The workers who ingested small quantities of paint often developed cystic and necrotic changes of the bones, which caused pains and led to easy fracture. Sometimes the changes progressed and cancer of the bones appeared, often fifteen years or more after the first exposure to the radioactive substance.

The workers in the uranium mines of Schneeberg and Joachimsthal during the last century were liable to die in middle life from a disease of the lungs which has been recognized as cancer of the lungs. About one half the miners who had died up to 1939 had contracted lung cancer. The radium and other radioactive elements in the uranium ore produce the gas radon as a decay product. The radon causes the air of the mines to be highly radioactive, and the inhalation of the air permits the solid decay products of radon to deposit in the lungs. The average radiation exposure of the lungs of these miners has been estimated to be about 1000 roentgens.

Exposure of cells to radiation may kill the cells. The cells of the bone marrow, which produce the constituents of blood, may be killed by radiation in sufficient number to give rise to anemia. Many people exposed to radiation in the course of their work show a fall in the numbers of red cells, white cells, and platelets in the blood. The disease in which the bone marrow is deficient in such a way that it cannot produce enough red cells is called aplastic anemia. Some cases of aplastic anemia have been reported among radiologists, patients who have been treated with large amounts of x-radiation, and survivors of the atomic bomb blasts at Hiroshima and Nagasaki.

Cataracts, opacity of the lens of the eye, have been observed to occur in patients who have been exposed to x-rays, in the survivors of Hiroshima and Nagasaki, and in physicists who have been exposed to neutron radiation during the operation of cyclotrons or the execution of experiments with fissionable material. There is no doubt whatever that ionizing radiation produces cancer and other diseases when the exposure is large. The argument that we have given above, based on the effect of the tiny bullets in changing the important molecules that control the cells, suggests that it also has a proportionate effect in producing some cases of these diseases even when the amount is small.

Leukemia

Leukemia is a disease in which there is an abnormal production of the white cells of the blood, the leucocytes. At the present time it is always fatal, although in some cases death may be delayed for many years. There are several kinds of leukemia. Usually there is an increase in the number of the white cells in the blood, with many of the cells immature. Sometimes the number of white cells falls below normal, because the cells are not liberated from the site of their formation. This disease is called aleukemic leukemia.

A thorough discussion of leukemia and ionizing radiation has been published by Dr. E. B. Lewis, Professor of Biology in the California Institute of Technology (*Science,* 17 May 1957; *The Nature of Radioactive Fallout and Its Effects on Man,* page 961). Much information has also been given in the report of the British Medical Research Council for presentation to Parliament ("The Hazards to Man of Nuclear and Allied Radiations," reprinted in *The Na-*

ture of Radioactive Fallout and Its Effects on Man, page 1553).

Careful studies have been made of the incidence of leukemia in the survivors of the atomic bomb burst over Hiroshima and Nagasaki. These survivors received exposures ranging from a few roentgens to 1000 roentgens or more.

They are divided into four groups, as shown in Table 3. The first group, A, consists of the estimated 1870 survivors who were within 1 kilometer of the hypocenter (the point on the surface of the earth directly below the bomb when it exploded). There were very few survivors in this zone, and they received a large amount of radiation.

The second group, B, consists of the 13,730 survivors between 1.0 and 1.5 kilometers from the hypocenter, the third, C, of the 23,060 between 1.5 and 2.0 kilometers, and the fourth, D, of the 156,400 over 2.0 kilometers from the hypocenter.

The survivors of zones A, B, and C have been dying of leukemia during the period of careful study, the eight years from 1948 to 1955, at an average rate of about 9 per year. The numbers of confirmed cases of leukemia for the four zones during the period of eight years are given in the fifth column of Table 3. It is seen that many more cases of leukemia occurred in the 15,600 survivors of zones A and B than in the 156,400 survivors of zone D, who received much less radiation. There is no doubt that the increased incidence is to be attributed to the exposure to radiation.

The estimated average radiation exposure for each of the four zones is given in the third column. These values are in the unit rem, which for our purposes can be taken equal to roentgens. The survivors of zone A received an estimated average of 650 roentgens, those of zone B, 250; those of zone C, 25, and of zone D, 2.5. In column six there are given the number of cases of leukemia that would have been expected to occur from causes other than the radiation from the bomb explosions. These numbers have been obtained by taking zone D as the control.

The seventh column contains the number of cases of leukemia attributed to the radiation.

The results given in Table 3 are shown graphically in Figure 5, which is redrawn from a figure presented by Dr. Lewis before the Special Congressional Subcommittee on Radiation. To within the reliability of the numbers, the incidence of leukemia in the three populations A, B, and C is proportional to the estimated dose of radiation, even for class C, in which the estimated dose is only 25 roentgens.

From this information and information about the occurrence of leukemia in children treated with x-rays for enlargement of the thymus gland and in adult patients treated with x-radiation for control of the disease ankylosing spondylitis, Dr. Lewis concluded that the probability of radiation-induced leukemia is about 2 per million per roentgen year. This means that exposure of a population of 10,000 people to 100 roentgens of radiation would be expected to lead to two cases of leukemia in the population during each succeeding year.

Some information is also given by the observed incidence of leukemia in American radiologists. A study of a population of about 1850 American radiologists showed that 17 had died of leukemia, whereas only three deaths from leukemia would have been expected if the death rate were normal. The difference is so great that it must be significant; something is causing the radiologists to con-

Table 3

Incidence of Leukemia among the Combined Exposed Populations of Hiroshima and Nagasaki, January 1948 to September 1955

(After E. B. Lewis)

Zone	Distance from hypocenter (kilometers)	Average radiation dose (rem)	Estimated population of exposed survivors (1950)	Number of confirmed cases of leukemia	Number of normally expected cases	Number of cases attributed to radiation
A	0–0.999	650	1,870	18	0	18
B	1.000–1.499	250	13,730	41	2	39
C	1.500–1.999	25	23,060	10	4	6
D	2.000 & over	2.5	156,400	26	–	–

tract leukemia. It is reasonable to attribute the excess of 14 deaths from leukemia to the repeated small exposures to x-radiation received by them in the course of the practice of their profession.

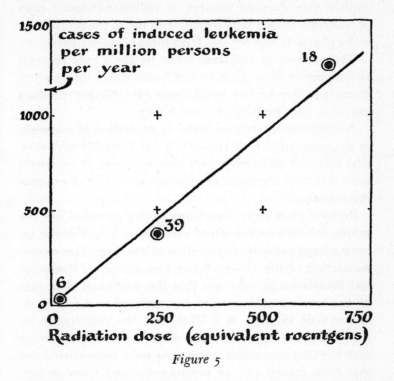

Figure 5

There is much uncertainty about the average exposure to radiation that these radiologists received. An upper limit, 660 roentgens, would be given by the maximum dose rate for radiologists set in 1931 by the United States National Committee on Radiological Protection. This rate was reduced by one half in 1936 and reduced again by one half in 1949, and it is hence probable that the average

89

exposure is somewhat less than this maximum. An average exposure of 300 roentgens, approximately that corresponding to the maximum dose set by the United States National Committee on Radiological Protection in 1936, would explain the observed number of radiation-induced cases of leukemia among radiologists, with use of the probability of incidence found for the Hiroshima-Nagasaki survivors.

The analysis of leukemia made by Dr. Lewis presents at the present time the most significant direct information about whether or not small doses of radiation produce cancer in the irradiated human being.

A simple interpretation of the six extra cases of leukemia in the population C of Hiroshima and Nagasaki survivors, who received an average radiation exposure of 25 roentgens, is that 25 roentgens of radiation is enough to produce the disease.

Perhaps even more significant to this question are the results for radiologists. Only rarely does a radiologist receive a large exposure to radiation at one time. The recommendation of the United States Committee on Radiological Protection in 1931 was that the maximum dose rate be not over 0.2 roentgen per day, reduced to 0.1 in 1936, and to 0.05 in 1949. It is likely that the radiologists received doses of not more than about 0.1 roentgen during each working day, and that it is these small individual doses that have caused the 14 radiation-induced cases of leukemia among them during the period of the study, 1938 to 1952. The situation with leukemia among radiologists is then not at all similar to that of the production of acute radiation sickness, which is caused by a single large dose but not by the same amount of radiation in small doses. Instead it is similar to the genetic effect, where it is known that a series of small doses causes the same number of mutations as the same amount of radiation in a large dose. The induction of leukemia by a series of small doses among American radiologists is roughly quantitatively the same as the induction of leukemia by a single large dose in the Hiroshima-Nagasaki survivors.

I conclude that it is highly probable that small doses as well as large doses of radiation cause leukemia in human beings. I accept, as the best value available, the conclusion by Dr. Lewis that the probability of developing leukemia during each year after exposure to a dose of radiation is 2 per million per roentgen of exposure.

An independent estimate was made by the Indian scientists S. K. Mazumdar and A. Nagaratnam (*The Nature of Radioactive Fallout and Its Effects on Man,* page 1685). Using essentially the same information as used by Dr. Lewis, they reached the conclusion that ionizing radiation produces leukemia at the rate of approximately 3 cases per million per year per roentgen of exposure. This is 50 percent higher than the estimate made by Dr. Lewis.

Dr. Lewis pointed out that his estimate of the incidence of leukemia produced by radiation, assuming that it holds also for small doses of radiation, leads to the conclusion that between 10 percent and 20 percent of the cases of leukemia observed in the United States are produced by background radiation. About 10,000 cases of leukemia are reported per year in the United States, according to Dr. Lewis. This corresponds to about 150,000 per year in the world, of which between 15,000 and 30,000 are to be attributed to cosmic rays and natural radioactivity.

Bone Cancer

Cancer of the bone is a disease that usually leads to death in a short time unless it can be eliminated by surgical treatment, such as amputation. Its spontaneous occurrence is less than that of leukemia. About 2000 deaths from cancer of the bone are reported each year in the United States, as compared with about 10,000 from leukemia, and we may assume that about 30,000 people die from cancer of the bone each year in the world, as compared with about 150,000 from leukemia.

It is known that an increased incidence of cancer of the bone results from exposure to large amounts of radiation. Many deaths have been reported among patients who were given radium compounds internally for the treatment of mental disease or for various rheumatic and other infections, or who drank radioactive water for its presumed aid to health at a time when the dangers of ingestion of radium were not appreciated. Many have been reported also in workers in industry who ingested radium, mesothorium, and radiothorium while painting the dials of watches and clocks with luminous paint. An increased incidence has also been reported for groups of people who have received large exposure to x-radiation for therapeutic purposes.

Statistical information permitting a reliable estimate of the dependence of the incidence of bone cancer on the amount of radiation is not available. A few cases of bone cancer have been observed among the Hiroshima-Nagasaki survivors. They are so small in number, however, as to permit as the only conclusion that the incidence of bone cancer due to radiation is somewhat smaller than that of leukemia.

I shall assume that background radiation causes about the same fraction of all cases of bone cancer as of leukemia, which has been estimated by Dr. Lewis to be 10 to 20 percent, and that small amounts, as well as large amounts, of radiation have a proportional probability of causing bone cancer. With this assumption, the number of cases of bone cancer expected to result from fallout radioactivity would be about one fifth the number of cases of leukemia.

Radiation and Life Expectancy

The probability of death is increased by exposure to radiation. One hundred roentgens of full-body radiation is estimated to cause a decrease of life expectancy in man of 500 to 1000 days; that is, a year and one half to three years.

This estimate, that life expectancy is decreased by five days to ten days per roentgen of exposure, is the one made by Dr. Hardin B. Jones, Professor of Medical Physics and Physiology in the University of California in Berkeley. It agrees reasonably well with estimates made by other authorities. The estimate is based upon observations and experiments of many types, including the observed mortality rate of Hiroshima-Nagasaki survivors and of other populations of human beings who have received large amounts of radiation. Also much work has been done upon animals. It has been found that the fraction of life span lost per unit of radiation exposure is essentially the same for a number of species of animals, including the mouse, the rat, the guinea pig, the rabbit, and man.

In discussing the results obtained from the studies of animals, Dr. Jones pointed out (*The Nature of Radioactive*

Fallout and Its Effects on Man, page 1100 on) that a unit of radiation exposure, regardless of the intensity and the duration of the exposure, produces approximately the same relative disturbance to body structure in adults of all mammalian species, and continued "On the human life span scale these effects of radiation summarized from small-animal data suggest that one roentgen of radiation exposure is equivalent to fifteen days of physiologic aging." He pointed out that many different estimates give values of one to thirty days per roentgen of radiation exposure, and that the probable value for human beings is in the range between five and ten days per roentgen.

We can understand why exposure of the human body to radiation has an effect of causing an increase in the physiologic age. One roentgen exposure of the body causes an average of one thousand ions to be formed in each cell of the body. Most of these ions may be expected to produce abnormal molecules and some of these changed molecules may be important to the cell. Some of the cells may have a changed molecule such as, in the course of time, to cause the cell to proliferate into a cancerous growth. Others may have changed molecules produced by the radiation such as to cause them to function in a less satisfactory way than normal cells, perhaps in the way corresponding to the process of aging. Inasmuch as every bit of radiation produces ions independently of every other bit—each of the bullets of radiation is independent of others in its powers of ionization—we can understand why the aging effect may be strictly proportional to the amount of radiation, and why, with 100 roentgens producing a decrease in life expectancy of 500 to 1000 days, one roentgen can produce a decrease in life expectancy of five to ten days.

Part of the decreased life expectancy is due to the induction of leukemia. According to the analysis made by Dr. Lewis, the probability that one roentgen of radiation will produce leukemia in a human being is greater if the exposure is made when he is a child than if it is made when he is old. If we assume that the exposure is distributed over the lifetime of one man, taken to be 60 years, we find that on the average he loses twenty years from his normal life expectancy in case that he contracts leukemia as a result of irradiation. The estimate made by Dr. Lewis of the probability of incurring leukemia any year after receiving one roentgen of exposure is 2 per million. This leads to a decrease in life expectancy of 0.4 days for one roentgen of exposure during a lifetime, to which we add a decrease of about 0.1 day for bone cancer. Accordingly the prediction of the probability of producing the two diseases leukemia and bone cancer accounts for half a day decrease in life expectancy per roentgen of exposure. The remaining decrease in life expectancy giving the total five to ten days estimated as most probable by Dr. Hardin Jones may be due to the incurrence of other forms of cancer and to the increased probability of death from various other diseases as a result of the physiologic aging of the cells caused by the little bullets of radiation.

The background radiation, from cosmic rays and natural radioactivity, amounts to about 6 roentgens in 60 years, and is predicted, by the arguments just given, to cause a decrease in life expectancy of 30 to 60 days.

It must be pointed out that a decrease in life expectancy of five to ten days from one roentgen of radiation does not mean that every human being receiving the one roentgen of radiation would die five to ten days earlier than he would otherwise. What it means is that some of them would die ten or twenty or thirty years earlier than they would if they had not received the radiation, whereas others might live their normal life span.

Is There a Threshold?

In our discussion of genetic and somatic effects of radiation we have had to say from time to time that there does not exist rigorous proof that the effect of small amounts of radiation in producing mutations and in producing leukemia, bone cancer, and other diseases is proportional to the amount of exposure, as is known to be the case for large amounts of radiation.

Although there is no rigorous proof for the genetic effects, I believe that every geneticist who has expressed an opinion about the matter has stated that he believes that even very small amounts of radiation, such as the background radiation, cause mutations, and that the mutation rate is in fact proportional to the amount of radiation exposure of the reproductive organs.

We have given above an outline of some of the evidence indicating that for the production of leukemia and bone cancer there is similar proportionality to the radiation exposure, and that small amounts of radiation, the background radiation plus fallout radioactivity and other doses of radiation to which people all over the world are subjected, produce these diseases with a probability proportional to the amount of radiation.

I believe that one of the strongest arguments in support of this belief is the argument based on the nature of the damage done by the little bullets of radiation. A single bullet may damage a molecule in a cell so as to cause it to lead to a cancerous growth, in a way resembling the way in which a gene can be damaged by a single bullet of

96

radiation so as to cause it ultimately to lead to the birth of a defective child.

A strong piece of direct evidence is that leukemia is known to be produced in radiologists by a succession of small doses of radiation, which seem to have essentially the same effect in producing leukemia as an equal amount of radiation administered in a single dose.

It is not surprising that many scientists who have a background of experience such as to make their opinions significant agree that it is highly probable that small amounts of radiation, as well as large amounts, produce leukemia and bone cancer and other diseases and cause a shortening of life expectancy.

Of the leading scientists who testified before the Special Congressional Subcommittee on Radiation in its hearings in May and June 1957, nearly every one expressed the opinion that it is probable that small doses of radiation produce these diseases and cause a decrease in life expectancy. Scientists testifying to this effect include Dr. H. J. Muller, Professor of Zoology in Indiana University, Dr. Hardin Jones, Professor of Medical Physics and Physiology in the University of California in Berkeley, Dr. E. B. Lewis, Professor of Biology in the California Institute of Technology, and Dr. Ernest Pollard, Professor of Biophysics in Yale University.

Also, in the 1956 report on "The Hazards to Man of Nuclear and Allied Radiations," presented by the Medical Research Council of Great Britain for presentation to Parliament, the opinion is expressed, after a discussion of the evidence, that "On the whole the experiments seem in favor of a proportionality between the frequency of tumours produced in a given length of time and the amount of radioactive material in the body even at low dose levels."

This report was prepared by a committee of the leading scientists and medical research men of Great Britain.

On the other hand, some of the witnesses at the Congressional hearings expressed their belief that small amounts of radiation do not produce leukemia or bone cancer or other diseases, and do not cause a shortening in life expectancy. They said that they believed that there is a threshold to the carcinogenic effect of radiation; the threshold is the amount of radiation that a human being can receive without any chance whatever of production of disease.

The question of interest is whether or not there is a threshold higher than about 6 roentgens, the amount received by a human being as natural background radiation in a period of sixty years—the fallout radioactivity is, of course, added to the background radiation, so that a threshold lower than the background radiation would not prevent the fallout radioactivity from causing damage to the average human being.

Dr. Shields Warren is a physician who is a pathologist in New England Deaconess Hospital, Boston, and who was from 1947 to 1952 Director of the Division of Biology and Medicine of the Atomic Energy Commission and is now a member of the Advisory Committee. In his testimony he said that he was firmly convinced that radiation will produce mutations, that the estimates made by the majority of geneticists are reasonable and sound estimates, and that there is no threshold for damage to the hereditary material and no recovery from injury to it (page 983): but that "With acute or chronic radiation there is what is called a threshold effect in body cells. In other words, because many cells can continue to function even though irradiated and many cells in the body can be repaired even though damaged, we find that at low levels of radiation, there is no observable effect" (page 981).

Dr. Austin M. Brues, who is director of the biological and medical research division of the Argonne National Laboratory, testified that we do not yet know whether there is a threshold for decreasing life expectancy and production of cancer by radiation, and that in his opinion "There are also good reasons from what we know about the nature of cancer to suspect that the hazard goes down faster than the initiating agent" (that is, that there is a threshold) (page 933).

Dr. Charles L. Dunham, a physician who is Director of the Division of Biology and Medicine of the U.S. Atomic Energy Commission, prepared a statement on "Fallout from Nuclear Weapons Testing" that was being distributed in July 1957 by Lewis Strauss, the Chairman of the Atomic Energy Commission, to people who had written to President Eisenhower about the hazards of testing nuclear weapons. In his statement Dr. Dunham said that "Most of the leading pathologists believe that a threshold dose of radiation exists below which exposure to radiation will not cause leukemia."

This statement by Dr. Dunham summarizes one aspect of the situation—that some pathologists believe that there is a threshold. On the other hand, many scientists with a background of experience in the field believe that it is likely that there is no threshold, no dose of radiation such that the probability that the radiation will induce leukemia or other form of disease is zero.

I think that it is the latter who are right about this question—the scientists who are working on the problems of the nature of disease and the nature of the mechanisms of production of disease.

I myself believe that it is highly probable that there is no threshold for the production of leukemia and bone cancer and some other diseases, and that there is no threshold for the shortening of life expectancy by radiation.

Even if there were a threshold of, say, 10 or 15 roentgens for the production of some of these diseases, some people would be caused to die of leukemia or other disease by the fallout radioactivity; there are many people, a considerable fraction of the world's population, who receive 20 roentgens or more during their lifetime. The estimate of the National Academy of Sciences-National Research Council Committee is that the average exposure of people in the United States from background radiation and medical x-rays amounts to about 7.3 roentgens in thirty years, or 14.6 roentgens in a lifetime of sixty years. Many people receive more than their share of medical x-rays, or receive exposure to radiation in the course of their work. It is probable that half the people in the United States receive more than 15 roentgens of exposure to radiation during their lifetime. For them, the effect of fallout radioactivity is to be superimposed on this total. Consequently, even if there is a threshold (which I consider unlikely), fallout radioactivity can be expected to produce leukemia and bone cancer in a considerable fraction of the world's population.

The Somatic Effects of Fallout from Bomb Tests

How much damage is being done to the health of human beings now living by the fallout radioactivity from the bomb tests that have been carried out and are being carried out?

We shall discuss the effects to be expected from fallout

radioactivity on the basis of the assumption that there is no threshold for the production of leukemia and some other diseases or for the shortening of life.

The principal culprit in causing damage to human beings now living is the radioactive nucleus strontium-90. Strontium-90 is formed (by way of krypton-90 and rubidium-90) in large amount; it constitutes about 3 percent of the fissioned uranium-235, plutonium-239, and uranium-238.

It falls to earth all over the world in the tropospheric and especially the stratospheric fallout. Its distribution is not uniform: there is somewhat less in the Southern Hemisphere than in the Northern Hemisphere, and there are some regions where the concentration of strontium-90 in the surface soil is far greater, ten times or even one hundred times greater, than in other regions; but we may make our calculations without significant additional uncertainty in the results by treating it as uniform.

Figure 6 shows the way in which the amount of strontium-90 has been increasing.

The element strontium is closely similar in its chemical nature to the element calcium, which is an important constituent of plants and animals. The strontium-90 is taken up by plants and animals together with calcium. The amount taken up depends upon the amount of calcium in the soil. In general, the ratio of strontium-90 to calcium in the plant is somewhat less than that in the soil, probably about one half.

All over the world, cows now eat grass containing strontium-90, and the strontium-90 is now present in the milk of all cows.

Human beings eat vegetables and drink milk—all of the vegetables and all of the milk in the world now contain strontium-90. The human beings build some of the ingested strontium-90 into their bones, where it stays throughout the lifetime of the individual. The ratio of strontium-90 to calcium in human bones is about one

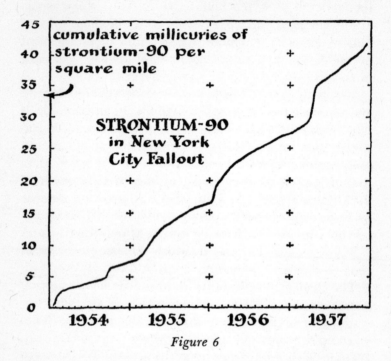

Figure 6

half of the ratio for the milk that they drink and about one twelfth of the ratio for the soil on which the vegetables and grass are grown.

Strontium-90 is a terrible poison—a poison that did not exist in the world, except for a few stray atoms in uranium and thorium minerals, a few years ago. One teaspoonful of this poison, distributed equally among all the people in the world, would kill all of them within a few years. When a single superbomb such as the 1 March 1954 bomb is detonated, about a thousand times this amount is thrown up into the air, to be distributed over the surface of the earth. It is fortunate that only a small part of it gets into the bodies of human beings.

The simplest way to discuss the effect of the testing of nuclear weapons is to consider the effect of a continued period of testing at the average rate for the past few years, 10 megatons equivalent of fission per year.

The estimate has been made by Dr. J. Laurence Kulp and his associates of Columbia University, on the basis of their analyses of strontium-90 in the bones of children and adults who have died in recent years, that if, after a long period of testing at the present rate, a steady state were finally to be set up the average concentration of strontium-90 in the bones of people of the world would be 20 micromicrocuries per gram of calcium (20 strontium units). This estimate agrees very closely with the estimates of other people; for example, Dr. Willard F. Libby in 1955 made the estimate 24 strontium units, and the estimate 30 strontium units, made by Dr. Wright Langham, is quoted in the 23rd Semiannual Report of the AEC.

The strontium-90 that is built into the bones continues to undergo radioactive decomposition year after year. Every minute some of the nuclei of strontium-90 undergo radioactive decay, shooting out beta particles, which damage the surrounding tissues. The product of the radioactive decay of a strontium-90 nucleus is a nucleus of yttrium-90, which itself then undergoes radioactive decay, usually within a few days, shooting out a still more energetic beta particle, which does still more damage to the surrounding tissues.

It is the bones and bone marrow and other tissues adjacent to the bones that are mostly subjected to damage by the radioactivity of the strontium-90 and its daughter nuclei. It is these parts of the human body in which damage causes leukemia and bone cancer. These parts of the body are subjected to a dose of about 0.050 roentgen each year by the strontium-90 present in concentration 0.020 to 0.030 strontium units.

If we make use of Dr. Lewis's estimate of the probability of production of leukemia by irradiation of the bone marrow and take sixty years as the average length of life of human beings, we calculate that when a steady state is set up, with testing of nuclear weapons continued at the present rate, there will be 8000 deaths from leukemia each year in the world (population 2,750,000,000), caused by strontium-90.

If the strontium-90 causes also a similar fractional increase in the incidence of bone cancer, as discussed above, the number of deaths from bone cancer induced by strontium-90 from the testing of nuclear weapons at the present rate, when a steady state is set up, is estimated to be 1600 per year.

An independent estimate has been made by Dr. H. B. Newcombe, head of the biology branch of Atomic Energy of Canada, Limited, Chalk River, Ontario (*Science,* 20 September 1957, page 549). He made use of the statistics about the incidence of osteosarcomas (bone cancer) in the province of Saskatchewan during the 13-year period from 1932 to 1944, and calculated an upper limit of predicted incidence of bone cancer from continued testing at the present rate. His upper limit is based on the assumption that the radiation-induced incidence is proportional to the intensity of the radiation and also the assumption that all the natural cases are due to background radiation.

The number that he calculates (converted to world population) is 22,000 cases per year, for the steady state.

We have assumed that radiation probably produces only 10 or 20 percent of the total number of cases. With this assumption, Dr. Newcombe's estimate is changed to 2200 to 4400 cases per year, somewhat larger than our estimate of 1600 cases per year.

We may take 2000, as a round number. Then we may say that about 10,000 deaths per year from both leukemia and bone cancer are predicted for the steady state corresponding to continued testing at the present rate.

The total decrease in life expectancy due to radiation is ten to twenty times that calculated for these two diseases. If we assume that the total decrease in life expectancy from fallout is ten times that due to leukemia and bone cancer, and that this decrease results from the death of a certain number of people about twenty years, on the average, before the normal time of death, as it is for leukemia, we obtain as the total number of deaths per year to be expected from continued testing at the present rate the number 100,000.

A single large bomb, a superbomb with perhaps a total of 15 or 20 megatons of nuclear explosive of which 10 megatons is fission, liberates the amount of fission products corresponding to the average rate of testing per year upon which the above calculation is made. Accordingly, our calculations give us the result that the testing of a single large superbomb, like the one that was detonated by the United States on 1 March 1954, causes an incidence of disease such as to lead to the death of 10,000 people by leukemia and bone cancer and possibly also 90,000 more by other diseases, a possible total of 100,000 deaths.

These figures are not exaggerations. The calculated

number of deaths by leukemia, as given above, corresponds closely with the results of a similar calculation made by Professor Lewis in his paper on leukemia and radiation. The Radiation Hazards Committee of the British Atomic Scientists Association, which numbered among its members several of the members of the Committee of the British Medical Research Council that made a report on radioactive fallout for submission to Parliament, stated in its report that "An H-Bomb of the type tested at Bikini in 1954, if exploded high in the atmosphere, may eventually produce bone cancers in 1000 people for every million tons of TNT of equivalent explosive" (*The Nature of Radioactive Fallout and Its Effects on Man,* page 1670). This estimate, which corresponds to 10,000 deaths by bone cancer for a superbomb with 10 megatons equivalent of fission, is about five times the estimate given above of 2000 deaths by bone cancer for such a bomb. This committee did not estimate the number of deaths from leukemia.

The total number of deaths, 100,000, that may be attributed to the Bikini bomb will be distributed over a period of many years; a few during the period immediately after the detonation of the bomb, a few during the following year, a few more during the next year, and so on, with a maximum number coming perhaps 40 years from now, when the children now living have grown to maturity and their bone marrow has the large chance of showing a malignant response to the radiation that has continued to impinge upon it from the strontium-90 that was built into it during the years subsequent to 1954.

If bomb testing were to be stopped now, the concentration of strontium-90 in the bones of children would continue to increase, reaching a maximum in about 1972. The effects of strontium-90 on our children will continue to increase during coming years, as the integrated amount of radiation to the bone marrow steadily increases.

The estimate that one large bomb, with 10 megatons equivalent of fission, causes, in the course of time, the death of 10,000 people by leukemia and bone cancer and possibly of 90,000 others by other diseases cannot be claimed to be an accurate one. There is some uncertainty, probably not greater than a factor of 2 or of $\frac{1}{2}$, in the expected average concentration of strontium-90 in the bones. There is, according to Dr. Lewis, an uncertainty by a factor of 3 or $\frac{1}{3}$ in the estimate of the effect of radiation in causing leukemia. If we accept these two uncertainties, we may say that it is likely that the number of deaths by leukemia and bone cancer from the testing of a large superbomb lies between 1700 and 60,000. If we accept the same uncertainties for other causes of shortening of life expectancy, the total number of people whose lives are expected to be cut off by the fallout from such a bomb is calculated to lie between 17,000 and 600,000.

There is also the possibility, which I consider to be a small one, that there is a threshold for radiation, below which no damage occurs. If there is such a threshold, only those individuals who receive during their lifetime a total amount of radiation from cosmic rays, natural radioactivity, medical x-rays, industrial exposure to radiation, and fallout greater than the threshold would respond to the fallout radioactivity, which is superimposed on the other types of radiation. In this case the estimates given above may be 10 times too large, or possibly 100 times too large; no one, however, contends that there would not be some individuals in the world who would be caused to die by the fallout radioactivity.

In the preceding chapter it was pointed out that, over

a period of thousands of years, the carbon-14 released by the bomb tests will do far more genetic damage than all the other radioactive products.

The corresponding calculation for leukemia is somewhat involved, but is straightforward. With Dr. Lewis's value for the probability of radiation-induced leukemia, it leads to 10,000 deaths by leukemia caused by the carbon-14 released by one year of testing (about 30 megatons, both fission and fusion). Thousands of cases of bone cancer and other kinds of cancer may also be caused by the carbon-14.

At the present time there is nobody in the world who can deny that there exists a real possibility that the lives of 100,000 people now living are sacrificed by each bomb test or series of bomb tests in which the fission products of 10 megatons equivalent of fission are released into the atmosphere.

In addition, there are the genetic effects of the fallout radioactivity. We have estimated the genetic effects as causing the birth, in future generations, of 15,000 seriously defective children for each 10 megatons equivalent of fission products released to the atmosphere, plus a much larger number of minor defects and a larger number of embryonic and neonatal deaths and stillbirths. It may well be that significant damage is done to as many as 100,000 individual human beings in future generations by the fallout radioactivity from one superbomb with 10 megatons equivalent of fission.

These numbers, 100,000 human beings now living and 100,000 in future generations, are small compared with the total number of human beings in the world. Each year about 30,000,000 people die in the world. We may say that the additional early death of 100,000 people caused by one year's testing is a small increase, only one third of

1 percent. We may describe it as a negligible increase—this depends upon one's definition of the word negligible. We may say that the increase is so small that it cannot be detected, as Dr. Libby has said.

In a letter that he wrote to a clergyman on 5 July 1957, in answer to a letter to President Eisenhower about the testing of nuclear weapons, Mr. Strauss, Chairman of the Atomic Energy Commission, said:

I believe the conclusion one must inevitably reach after balancing all factors is this—we have the choice of running a very small risk from testing or a risk of catastrophe which might result from a surrender of our leadership in nuclear armament which has been, we believe, the deterrent to aggression since 1945. The cause for most serious concern is not the effect of radiation resulting from tests to keep our weapons posture strong, but rather the effect of the infinite human devastation that would result from the massive use of nuclear weapons in warfare.

Recently at the hearings of the Congressional Joint Committee on Atomic Energy, Shields Warren, M.D., one of the country's most distinguished pathologists, Professor of Pathology at Harvard Medical School, Director of the Institute of Cancer Research at the New England Deaconess Hospital, Boston, and United States delegate to the United Nations Scientific Committee on the Effects of Atomic Radiation, closed his testimony with the following statement: "It would be inexcusable," he said, "for us to jeopardize our own safety and that of the rest of the free world in order to eliminate a risk of as low an order of magnitude as is constituted by a reasonable program of weapons testing."

I have a wife, a son, and three happy young grand-children. Yet I subscribe completely to Dr. Warren's views. I could not do so if I thought the welfare of my family was threatened more by fallout than by possible nuclear war. Many authorities in addition to Dr. Warren share his view and have families of their own to protect.

Mr. Strauss presumably does not really mean to say that he would be willing to jeopardize our safety and that of the rest of the free world if he thought that the welfare of his own family was threatened more by fallout than by possible nuclear war. He does not deny that the testing of nuclear weapons does damage to the health of human beings now living and to future generations. He expresses the belief that we have great cause to be concerned about the possibility of infinite human devastation that would result from the massive use of nuclear weapons in warfare. His statement suggests a willingness to gamble the health of the members of his family and of everybody else in order that we may "keep our weapons posture strong," in the belief that this will decrease the chance of outbreak of a nuclear war.

It is this belief that has probably led to the series of inadvertencies and misleading statements about fallout radioactivity and related questions that have been made by AEC spokesmen. These matters will be discussed in the following chapter.

In common with many others, I do not think that we achieve safety, in the nuclear world, by "keeping our weapons posture strong."

I believe that nuclear war, with its catastrophic conse-quences, possibly the destruction of the world, the end of civilization, must be averted. I believe that nuclear war will not be averted by a policy, followed by two great nations, of continued reliance on ever increasing force, ever greater powers of destruction.

I believe that the nations of the world that are carrying out the tests of nuclear weapons are sacrificing the lives of hundreds of thousands of people now living and of hundreds of thousands of unborn children, and that this sacrifice is unnecessary.

I believe that the way to avert nuclear war is to begin making safe, just, and effective international agreements; and that the first of these should include the stopping of the tests of all nuclear weapons.

6
What Are the Facts About Fallout?

You may be puzzled by apparent contradictions between statements made in the preceding chapters and statements that you may have read in other books and in magazines and newspapers. This chapter should help you to decide what the facts about fallout are.

The United States Atomic Energy Commission has published a great amount of information about the effects of nuclear explosions, and additional information has become available from other sources, such as the publications of Japanese scientists. Especially valuable are the two volumes *The Nature of Radioactive Fallout and Its Effects on Man,* the report of the hearings of the Special Congressional Subcommittee on Radiation.

Although there are some questions that have not yet been answered, there are many important facts about nuclear weapons, fallout, and biological effects of radiation that are accepted by all scientists. In his appearance before the Special Congressional Subcommittee on Radiation Dr. J. Laurence Kulp, who is an authority on strontium-90, said: "Finally, Mr. Chairman, if I might add one or two words as a citizen, rather than a scientist, for the record I would like to note three things: First, that I do not think the differences in the opinions of scientists, such as Dr. Libby and Dr. Pauling, are anywhere near as great as some of the newspaper accounts would lead us to believe. I believe that as far as scientific data are concerned, they are probably in rather close agreement. Dr. Libby has carefully said, or has pointed out that he is not saying that there is no risk, and Dr. Pauling has admitted that the radiation from strontium-90 is a very small fraction of the natural background. On these basic facts, all are agreed." (*The Nature of Radioactive Fallout and Its Effects on Man*, page 691.)

Yet the public has been given the impression that there is a great disagreement among scientists about the facts.

I think that the explanation of this situation is that the spokesmen for the Atomic Energy Commission have often made statements that seem to be misleading. Though many of the statements are true, they may convey the wrong impression. Sometimes the statements have turned out to be wrong.

Some examples of erroneous statements by representatives of the Atomic Energy Commission were discussed by Dr. Ralph E. Lapp in his testimony before the Special Congressional Subcommittee on Radiation. Dr. Lapp said (page 1279) that "Scientists, technicians, and officials of the AEC must present only reasoned and careful estimates of the hazards based upon factual knowledge. Reckless or non-substantiated statements do a disservice to the AEC and to the Nation." He then mentioned that Mr. Merril Eisenbud, manager of the New York Operations Office of the United States Atomic Energy Commission, had been quoted in an article entitled "Man Who Measures A-Fallout Belittles Danger" (*Sunday News,* New York, 20 March

113

1955) as follows: "The total fallout to date from all tests would have to be multiplied by a million to produce visible, deleterious effects except in areas close to the explosion, itself."

Mr. Eisenbud, who had said that he was talking about the immediate gamma radiation from the fallout which occurs in the Eastern United States within a matter of a day or so after a detonation in Nevada, was asked by Dr. Lapp and by the Chairman of the Subcommittee if he remembered how much radioactivity had fallen on the city of Troy, New York. He answered that something under 0.10 roentgen, which he estimated as only 0.01 roentgen, had fallen after a test held in Nevada in the spring of 1953. He said that there was a rain over the Troy-Albany area which coincided with a passage of a cloud from Nevada, so that a large percentage of this cloud was washed down. Dr. Lapp pointed out that a million times 0.01 roentgen would be 10,000 roentgens, and one of the Senators mentioned that 10,000 roentgens would kill everybody in the region.

We see that the statement made by Mr. Eisenbud, a representative of the Atomic Energy Commission, was not correct.

The Statements of Dr. Willard F. Libby

Dr. Willard F. Libby is a distinguished scientist (a physical chemist) who, after serving as Professor in the Institute of Nuclear Studies in the University of Chicago, has been a member of the Atomic Energy Commission itself since 1954. For much of this time he has been the only scientist among the members of the Atomic Energy Commission.

It is likely that a large part of the extensive scientific

information that has been gathered by the Atomic Energy Commission about fallout and its biological effects has resulted from the activities of Dr. Libby. I feel that he deserves great credit for these activities.

Dr. Libby has to be described as a thoughtful and careful scientist. Nevertheless, he has made many public statements that I consider to be misleading.

In his speech of 3 June 1955 he said that "However, as far as immediate or somatic damage to the health is concerned, the fallout dosage rate as of January 1 of this year in the United States could be increased 15,000 times without hazard."

This statement can hardly be described as correct. Ten hours after the detonation of a small fission bomb at the Nevada Test Site on 1 March 1955 the level of gamma radiation at St. George, Utah, was 0.004 roentgen per hour. Similar radiation levels have been reported for other cities in Utah and Nevada, and also in the Troy-Albany region of New York. They correspond to about 0.1 roentgen of fallout exposure within a period of one day.

If the inhabitants of these regions had received a fallout dosage 15,000 times greater, amounting to 1500 roentgens, they would have died within a few days of acute radiation sickness. Consequently the 15,000 increase cannot be said to be without hazard.

Another statement by Dr. Libby was reported in the *New York Herald Tribune* of 9 June 1957. On the previous day Dr. Libby had said that "There is no single provable case of any person being injured or seriously affected by any of the slightly extra radiation created in the United States by the tests." He did not amplify this statement.

I myself believe that this statement is, in a sense, accurate: when a man dies from leukemia or bone cancer there is no way of telling whether his disease was caused by fallout radiation or by cosmic rays or heredity or by some other natural cause, and when a defective child is born there is no way of proving that his genetic defect is to be attributed to fallout radiation rather than to some other cause. Hence no one person can be pointed out as having died from leukemia or bone cancer caused by fallout, no one child can be pointed out as being seriously defective because of fallout—there is no provable case, as Dr. Libby says.

And yet, Dr. Libby's statement misleads because it suggests to most readers that the fallout radiation does no harm.

The Denver Argument

One argument that has been used by spokesmen for the Atomic Energy Commission to "allay the fears of the people" about the effects of fallout is an argument based on a comparison of the incidence of leukemia and bone cancer in Denver with that in San Francisco and New Orleans.

The intensity of cosmic radiation in Denver, at an altitude of 5000 feet, is about 0.023 roentgen per year greater than at sea level, according to Dr. Libby. Dr. Libby gives the natural background radiation at sea level as 0.110 roentgen per year. Accordingly, if the natural radioactivity were the same in Denver as in San Francisco and New Orleans the average exposure of people to radiation from all natural sources would be 21 percent greater in Denver than in the other two cities.

It has been estimated by Dr. E. B. Lewis of the California Institute of Technology, in his careful study of radiation in relation to leukemia, that about 10 to 20 percent

116

of the cases of leukemia may be attributed to cosmic rays or natural radioactivity. Accordingly it might be expected that, if other factors were the same, the incidence of leukemia in Denver would be between 2 and 4 percent greater than that in San Francisco and New Orleans.

Dr. Libby has pointed out that there is no evidence from medical statistics that this increase in the incidence in leukemia or a similar increase in the incidence of bone cancer actually occurs in Denver in comparison with San Francisco and New Orleans. He presented his argument in an address given at the University of New Hampshire on 11 April 1957 and in an address delivered before the American Physical Society in Washington, D. C., on 26 April 1957 (pages 1517 and 1523 of *The Nature of Radioactive Fallout and Its Effects on Man*).

The argument is, however, misleading. It has no significance upon the question whether or not fallout radiation causes leukemia and bone cancer, because the medical statistics at the present time are not good enough to detect the predicted difference, and because other factors may hide this effect.

Let us quote from Dr. Libby's address of 26 April 1957: "Therefore, we must examine whether anything in our experience indicates that these differences (in cosmic ray intensity) are significant in terms of the occurrence of the principal effects expected of radiostrontium, namely leukemia and bone cancer. Now of course when one looks for such vital statistics, one finds that they are very hard to acquire. However, the National Institutes of Health and the Department of Health, Education, and Welfare have given us statistics for the occurrence of leukemia and bone cancer for the year 1947 for the three cities New Orleans, San Francisco and Denver."

117

Table 4

Occurrence of Bone Cancer and Leukemia
(New cases per year per 100,000 population)
(Reproduced from Dr. W. F. Libby)

	Bone cancer	Leukemia
Denver	2.4	6.4
New Orleans	2.8	6.9
San Francisco	2.9	10.3

"It is clear from this table," Dr. Libby went on to say, "that there is no obvious effect of altitude, and it is also clear that there are other factors which are noticeably more important than cosmic ray dosage. Of course there may still be a considerable effect of altitude hidden in large fluctuations caused by other factors, which presumably are largely unknown, and we cannot say that this *proves* anything. It does, however, give us some assurance from normal experience that the effect of 8 Sunshine Units will not cause a detectable increase in bone cancer or leukemia."

The reference to 8 Sunshine Units means 8 micromicrograms of strontium-90 per gram of calcium in the bones—this is about the equivalent of the increased intensity of the cosmic rays in Denver.

Dr. Libby is, of course, right in saying that this statistical argument does not prove anything. Nobody knows why there has been reported a larger incidence of bone cancer and leukemia in San Francisco than in Denver and New Orleans. It is possible that the medical statistics given in the table are so unreliable as to put the cities in the wrong order—the number of cases of bone cancer and leukemia in these cities in 1947 was so small that statistical fluctuations would cause each of the numbers in the table to be uncertain by one or two units, so that the differences cannot be considered to be very significant. Also, it is possible that the exposure to natural radioactivity—radium and potassium-40—is different in the different cities. It is not unlikely that the exposure to medical x-rays is significantly different in the different cities; it is with little doubt considerably larger in San Francisco than in the other two cities. It is probable that the average age of the people in Denver is less than that of the people in the other two cities, and the incidence of cancer increases with increasing age. And it may be that patients with these diseases are attracted to San Francisco and New Orleans by their medical facilities, and not to Denver.

Dr. Libby is right in saying that his argument does not prove anything.

However, he is wrong in then saying that it gives us assurance about the effect of strontium-90. An effect as large as a 10-percent increase of leukemia and bone cancer caused by cosmic rays in Denver obviously could be masked by whatever effects are responsible for the difference in the numbers.

Dr. Edward Teller and Dr. Albert Latter have included this argument in their article "The Compelling Need for Nuclear Tests," which was published in *Life* Magazine for 10 February 1958, and in their book *Our Nuclear Future*. After presenting the argument briefly, they stated that "The only thing these statistics prove is that radiation in small doses need not necessarily be harmful—indeed may conceivably be helpful."

119

This statement by Dr. Teller and Dr. Latter is more than a misleading statement; it is not valid.

Dr. Teller and Dr. Latter say that the statistics *prove* that radiation in small doses need not necessarily be harmful, may conceivably be helpful. *The statistics do not prove this in any way*—as Dr. Libby has said, *these statistics do not prove anything*.

Dr. Teller's Statements

Dr. Edward Teller is an able and experienced scientist who was born and educated in Hungary and who came to the United States in 1935. During recent years he has become well known to the people of the United States and of other countries as "The Father of the H-Bomb." He has been called in by President Eisenhower to discuss nuclear weapons, and he himself has made many public statements about nuclear weapons, fallout, the education of scientists in the U.S.S.R. and the U.S., and other topics.

Dr. Teller's public statements about fallout and its biological effects may be misunderstood by some readers. The discussion that is given in the following pages may help the reader to discover what the truth is. He might otherwise be confused by apparent contradictions between Dr. Teller's statements and the statements made in this book.

As a simple example, I may quote the statement made by Dr. Teller that "The worldwide fallout is as dangerous to human health as being one ounce overweight."

It would be hard to make a statement about fallout that is more easily misinterpreted than this one. What meaning does being one ounce overweight have? No scientist believes that being one ounce overweight causes a significant increase in the probability in having one's life cut short by leukemia or bone cancer or other disease—yet many scientists believe that fallout radioactivity increases the incidence of these diseases.

Dr. Teller's statement about being one ounce overweight is a ludicrous one, and it is a seriously misleading one, in that it gives the impression to the reader that the idea that fallout can shorten life expectancy is also ludicrous.

In making this statement Dr. Teller was discussing life expectancy on a statistical basis. But he made a serious error in the interpretation of the statistical information, such as to have caused him to overestimate by a factor of 1500 the statistical effect of being one ounce overweight.

I believe that if he wanted to discuss the statistical effect of being one ounce overweight (a pretty uncertain concept, in any case), the correct statement, which he should have made, is that "The world-wide fallout is 1500 times as dangerous to human health as being one ounce overweight." I have presented a paper to the National Academy of Sciences on "The Relation Between Longevity and Obesity in Human Beings," in which this question is discussed (Annual Meeting of the U.S. National Academy of Sciences, Washington, D. C., 28 April 1958, to be published in the *Proceedings of the National Academy of Sciences,* July 1958).

The erroneous statements in the issue of *Life* Magazine for 10 February 1958 begin on the cover. Here, in large letters, is the statement "Dr. Teller refutes 9000 scientists." According to the dictionary, the word refute means "To disprove and overthrow by arguments or proofs; to prove to be false or erroneous." In fact Dr. Teller did not show that any single statement in the petition presented by 9235 scientists to the United Nations was false or erroneous. He did not disprove and overthrow, by any valid argument, evidence, or proof, any part of the petition.

Following the example of *Life* Magazine in its statement on the cover of their issue of 10 February 1958, I shall from now on speak of Dr. Teller, rather than both authors, in discussing the article and book by Drs. Teller and Latter.

The way in which Dr. Teller underestimates the fallout risks can be illustrated by his figures on radiation due to strontium-90. After discussing strontium-90, which he properly calls a dangerous poison, and after mentioning that there is strong evidence that radiation such as that produced by strontium-90 increases the chance that a human being will contract the diseases bone cancer or leukemia during his lifetime, he says "This sounds frightening until one considers the slight amount of radiation we are subjected to from worldwide fallout." He then mentions that the strontium-90 that falls to the earth is absorbed by growing plants and reaches our bodies when we eat the plants or when we drink milk from cows that have grazed on radioactive grass. He mentions that the humans who absorb the greatest dosage of strontium-90 are young children—especially those in the northern part of the U.S., which is a region of maximum fallout. Then he says "Adults who reached mature growth before the atomic testing started are now getting about 0.0003 roentgen a year in their bones from strontium-90. Children who have grown up in an environment of strontium-90 are absorbing a larger dose, but it is still less than 0.002 roentgen a year (in addition, all of us receive a roughly equal amount from cesium-137). . . . If tests continue at the present rate, radiation levels might increase as much as five-fold."

The best information that we now have about strontium-

90 in the bones of man was published in the 7 February 1958 issue of the magazine *Science* by Dr. J. Laurence Kulp of the Lamont Geological Observatory of Columbia University and his colleagues Drs. W. R. Eckelmann and A. R. Schulert. Their results lead to the equilibrium level of 20 micromicrocuries of strontium-90 per gram of calcium, if testing is continued at the present rate. This corresponds to about 0.05 roentgen per year of radiation to the bones—not a five-fold increase, as Dr. Teller said, but a 25-fold increase over the present value for children, and a 167-fold increase over the present value for adults.

Dr. Teller's statement underestimates the future danger by a factor of 5, relative to children, or of 33, relative to adults.

Dr. Teller mentions that the people of Tibet have been exposed for generation after generation to a considerably larger amount of cosmic radiation than people who live at lower altitudes, and says "Yet genetic differences have not been noted in the humans of Tibet, or for that matter in any other living species there."

He surely knew, or should have known, that the increased amount of cosmic radiation in Tibet is such as to produce an estimated 15-percent increase in the incidence of seriously defective children in Tibet. Instead of 2 percent of the babies being born seriously defective because of bad genes, about 2.3 percent might be expected in Tibet. And he surely knew, or should have known, that there exist no medical statistics whatever for Tibet to permit one to say whether or not there are somewhat more defective children born there than in the United States.

This paragraph about Tibet in Dr. Teller's article in *Life* Magazine cannot strictly be said to be incorrect. It is true that genetic differences that might be attributed to

123

cosmic radiation have not been noticed in the humans of Tibet or other living species there; but it is also true that they have not been looked for. Thus the paragraph has to be described as seriously misleading.

In a television debate with Dr. Teller on 20 February 1958 I said to him that this argument was a red herring, designed to mislead the reader, and I asked him why he had included it in the *Life* article. He said that the argument had been included in order to "quiet excessive fears."

He also made a statement in the article and the book about the American servicemen and Marshallese islanders who had been exposed to fallout radioactivity after the Bikini explosion of 1 March 1954. He mentioned that 28 American servicemen on the island of Rongerik received an average dosage of about 78 roentgens, 18 Marshallese islanders on Ailinginae received 69 roentgens, 157 on Utirik received 14 roentgens, and 64 on Rongelap received an average of 175 roentgens. (They narrowly escaped a much heavier dosage. Ten miles to the north on the island they would have received 400 roentgens, which would have given them only a 50-50 chance of survival, and on the northern tip of the island, thirty miles away, the dosage would have been over 2000 roentgens, which would have meant certain death.)

He mentioned that the 64 native inhabitants of Rongelap complained at first of nausea, fever, stomach-ache, itching skin and burning sensations, skin lesions, and loss of hair, but that after six months the lost hair had grown out again and the skin lesions had healed. He mentioned that there were four pregnancies among the Rongelap women at the time of the exposure, and that, although one baby was born dead, the other three were quite normal. Then he said "The important fact is that today, more than three years after the accident, all of the Marshallese and American victims seem to be fully recovered from a dosage of radioactivity far greater than any humans are ever likely to be subjected to again from a bomb test. Although long-term effects are being carefully watched for, no malignancies or cases of leukemia have shown up to date."

But the probability of incidence of leukemia or bone cancer after exposure to radiation, as discussed in Chapter 5, is such that the exposure received by these 267 human beings would be expected to cause about one death by leukemia or bone cancer among them in 25 years. The fact that none of the American servicemen or Marshallese islanders has died of leukemia or bone cancer during three years has accordingly little value as evidence.

The Fable of the Wrist Watch

Dr. Willard F. Libby in an article in *Science* (**122,** 57, 1955; also *The Nature of Radioactive Fallout and Its Effects on Man,* page 1460) wrote: "A wrist watch worn 24 hours per day that has a luminous dial assumed to have 1 microcurie of radium per watch—a figure perhaps slightly larger than the average—would give the central body, including the sex organs (at average distance of 1 foot), a dosage of about 0.040 roentgen per year."

Dr. Teller then wrote in his book and his *Life* Magazine article that a wrist watch with a luminous dial subjects us to much more radiation than we get from fallout. He amplified this statement in a chart, as shown in the figure on the following page.

The chart carries the caption "Radiation danger to the average person from various sources is shown in chart in roentgens per year (figures at bottom)." The effect of wrist

125

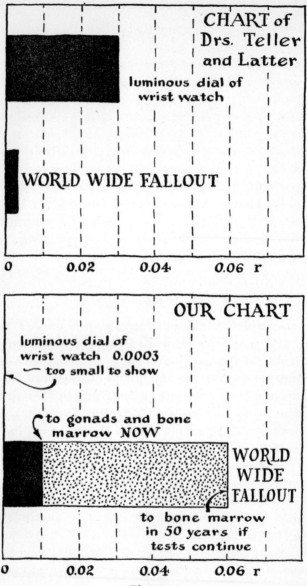

Figure 7

watches is given as 0.030, and that of fallout as 0.003 roentgen per year.

Hence Dr. Teller contends that the radiation danger to the average person is ten times as great from wrist watches as from fallout.

He overestimates the wrist watch effect greatly—I think that he has taken it to be about 100 times as great as it actually is for the average person in the United States, and about 500 times as great as it actually is for the average person in the world.

Dr. Libby said that his 1 microcurie of radium might be a larger amount than that for the average wrist watch. The British Report of the Medical Research Council for presentation to Parliament (*The Nature of Radioactive Fallout and Its Effects on Man,* page 1593) says that measurements and calculations give one fifth of a microcurie of radium for the average wrist watch.

Dr. Libby's calculation was for a watch one foot from the gonads, 24 hours a day, throughout the life of the person. I think that 16 or 18 inches is a better distance, and that watches are often worn only a part of each day and during only a part of a lifetime. These two circumstances probably introduce a correction factor of $\frac{1}{4}$.

Moreover, only about 15 percent of the people in the United States and Europe wear wrist watches with radium dials, and probably less than 3 percent of the people in the world. This fact gives a correction factor of 0.15 or 0.03.

Dr. Teller cannot contend that his chart was to show the radiation exposure of those people wearing wrist watches, rather than the average person. First, the legend to his figure reads "Radiation danger to the average person." Second, he gives in the chart a representation of the value for medical x-rays which is the average value for all people in the United States, and not the much higher value for those who receive x-ray treatment.

The exposure of the gonads of the average person in the United States to wrist watch radioactivity is hence about $0.040 \times \frac{1}{5} \times \frac{1}{4} \times 0.15 = 0.0003$ roentgen per year. The exposure for the average person in the world is about 0.00006 roentgen per year.

The value given by Dr. Teller for radiation danger to the average person from luminous dials of wrist watches, 0.030 roentgen per year, is 100 times too large for the average person in the United States, and 500 times too large for the average person in the world! Compare our chart with the Teller-Latter chart (Fig. 7).

Both in their book and in their article in *Life* Magazine Dr. Teller and Dr. Latter include the statement "Since the people are the sovereign power in a democracy, it is of the greatest importance that they should be honestly and completely informed about all the relevant facts." This statement seems to be out of place.

The Safe Nuclear Bomb

In his book and his *Life* Magazine article Dr. Teller shows a photograph of five intrepid Air Force officers standing unsheltered while a nuclear bomb explodes 19,000 feet directly above their heads. They experienced only a wave of warmth, a loud noise, and no significant rise in radioactivity.

Can we conclude from this that nuclear bombs are safe? No! Such a conclusion is not justified.

If the bomb had been exploded at 1900 feet, rather than 19,000 feet, the immediate radiation would have been 100 times as great, and the officers might not have been able to live through the experience. The Hiroshima bomb was detonated at an altitude of 2200 feet.

Dr. Teller does not say how big the bomb was. It was probably smaller than one kiloton. He does not say that the bombs that are ready for use in attack on the U.S. and the U.S.S.R. are 10,000 or 20,000 times more powerful. The officers could not stand unharmed under such a bomb.

One does not have to be an H-bomb scientist or to have secret information to know that Dr. Teller's miniscule bomb was a simple fission bomb, made of plutonium (possibly mixed with some uranium-235). It was a "dirty" bomb, releasing much radioactivity, in relation to its explosive energy. Yet Mr. Leonard Engel, in his review of the Teller-Latter book in *The New York Times Book Review* for 23 March 1958, was misled into describing this bomb as showing the progress that has been made in developing "clean" nuclear explosives!

MPD and MPC

Amounts of radiation and of radioactive elements are often compared with the Maximum Permissible Dose (MPD) of radiation and the Maximum Permissible Concentration (MPC) of radioactive elements. The significance of these quantities is still uncertain, and there has been much misunderstanding of their meaning.

Beginning in 1928, the International Commission on Radiological Protection has set standards and procedures for protection from radiation and radioactive materials on an international basis. The same work has been done for the United States since 1929 by the National Committee on Radiation Protection and Measurement. From time to time recommendations are made by these organizations about the permissible doses for external radiation and internal radiation and for protection against high-energy radiation and radioactive elements in general.

The MPD and the MPC are not the amounts that are known to be safe, or to cause no harm whatever to human beings and to future generations. They are, instead, values that do not cause obvious harm. This fact is reflected in the history of the development of these standards of protection.

In 1925, when the International Commission on Radiological Units and Measurements was established by the First International Congress of Radiology, the MPD was set as an amount that caused a certain amount of erythema (redness of the skin), which is estimated to correspond to 50 to 100 roentgens per year. In 1934 the International Commission on Radiological Protection adopted the MPC as 0.2 roentgen per day, equal to 72 roentgens per year. In 1935 the National Committee on Radiological Protection adopted the value of 0.1 roentgen per day, equal to 36 roentgens per year. In 1947 the NCRP lowered the MPD to 0.3 roentgen per week (15 roentgens per year), and in 1957 it was lowered again to 0.1 roentgen per week (5 roentgens per year). The change from 0.3 roentgen per week to 0.1 roentgen per week for people exposed to radiation in the course of their professional work was adopted by the AEC in December 1957.

The present MPC is accordingly only one fourteenth of that adopted in 1934.

The significance of the 1934 MPD and the present MPD can be estimated by consideration of the life-shortening effect. The life-shortening effect is with little doubt somewhere within the range of one to twenty days per roentgen. If we take the minimum value, one day per roentgen, the life-shortening effect of the MPD in 1934 was 72 days for each year of exposure, about eight years for a worker who received a maximum exposure throughout his active period of 40 years of employment. The present MPD corresponds to seven months decrease in life expectancy, if the life-shortening effect is for one day per roentgen, for a worker who receives the MPD over a period of 40 years, and correspondingly more if the life-shortening effect is larger (3 years if it is 5 days per roentgen).

It is likely that a major part of the life-shortening effect results from the increased incidence of leukemia and other diseases that cut life short by perhaps 20 years. If all of the life-shortening effects were of this sort, and the magnitude were one day per roentgen, it would be expected that one worker out of 35 who received the MPD over a period of 40 years would die 20 years early as a result of radiation injury, with the MPD at its present level.

There are, of course, uncertainties about these estimates, but there is little doubt that they give an approximate indication of the significance of radiation damage corresponding to the MPD.

The MPC of strontium-90 has been set at 1000 strontium units (micromicrocuries per gram of calcium). This concentration of strontium-90 irradiates the bones and bone marrow by approximately 1 to 3 roentgens per year. The damage to health that can be expected from it is approximately that described above, if small amounts of radiation have a similar effect to large amounts, but proportionally to the dose.

The recommendation has been made that the values of the MPD and MPC should be smaller for large populations, such as the population of the world as a whole, than for industrial workers and other small populations. Suggested values are one-tenth to one-fiftieth of the values for small groups of people. The argument involved is that a dose of radiation or a concentration of radioactive element that seriously damages the health of one out of, say, one hundred recipients might be tolerated in a small group, of the order of hundreds in size, but that it should not be tolerated for the whole population of the United States or of the world, because it would lead to damage to millions or tens of millions of individual human beings. Similarly, a gonad dose that increases by some amount the mutation rate for a few human beings in the world would not seriously damage the pool of human germ plasm, but a gonad dose of, say, 50 roentgens for the entire population of the world would double the mutation rate, and, if continued, would double the number of seriously defective children born in future generations.

It is not justified to speak of the MPD or MPC as a safe amount of exposure, or an amount of exposure that does no damage. An example of the misunderstanding that has arisen is provided by an article by correspondent Gladwyn Hill of *The New York Times* (9 June 1957). In discussing some tests of small nuclear weapons at the Nevada Test Area, Mr. Hill said that the amount of exposure of people in that neighborhood to fallout radioactivity and to radiation from the tests was far less than the amount 50 roentgens which had been set by the Committee on Biological Effects of Atomic Radiation of the National Academy of Science-National Research Council as the amount that does no harm. This was an error in interpretation; the Committee did not describe 50 roentgens, nor 10 roentgens, as an amount that does no harm, but instead said that any additional radiation is undesirable, that genetic harm is proportional to the total dose.

The best course that we can follow is that recommended by the Committee: *keep the dose as low as you can.*

7

The Nature of
Nuclear War

What would happen if a nuclear war were to break out?

It is likely that the disaster would be a sudden one. Perhaps most of the damage would be done within one day. During this one day there might be so effective a destruction of the nations with nuclear weapons that the war would then be over. Probably, however, fighting would drag on for some time, with further destruction done to the world.

No matter how the war would end, it would begin with a bang!

It might start by accident—the accidental detonation of a thermonuclear bomb over Moscow, for example, which would start the catastrophic series of retaliatory and counter-retaliatory attacks.

The military leaders of the world seem to be convinced that effectiveness in waging nuclear war requires vigilance and readiness to attack without delay—a delay of a few hours might render much of the striking power ineffective.

Within a few hours there would be thousands of great bombers, guided missiles, and ballistic missiles speeding toward their targets in the United States, the British Isles,

133

and all of the countries surrounding the Soviet Union from which nuclear attack might come. Each plane and each rocket would carry its great bomb, a hydrogen bomb or a superbomb with 5 or 10 or 20 megatons of explosive energy. And within a few hours thousands of these great bombs would also be speeding toward their targets within the Soviet Union.

General Lauris Norstad, NATO Commander, has said that "The United States has the power to inflict absolute destruction on Russia." We have to believe also that Russia has the power to inflict absolute destruction on the United States.

Some of the missiles might be shot down before reaching their targets. There is no hope, however, that really effective methods of defense against these missiles can be developed. It would be optimistic to believe that as many as one half of the bombs could be prevented from reaching their targets.

Several hundred, perhaps as many as two thousand, great bombs would explode over cities and other targets in the United States.

For example, three or four 20-megaton superbombs might explode over Los Angeles. A 20-megaton bomb is one thousand times as powerful as the Hiroshima bomb or the Nagasaki bomb. The cities of Hiroshima and Nagasaki were smashed flat over an area about two miles in diameter around the point below the bursting bomb. With a 20-megaton bomb the linear dimensions of the blasted area would be about ten times as great; the city would be smashed flat within a circle about twenty miles in diameter under each bomb.

Many people would be killed by the shock wave from the explosion. And each bomb would produce a great fireball with surface temperature greater than that of the sun. The heat from this fireball would burn to death many of the people within the circle twenty miles in diameter—nearly all of those who were not protected in some way. Many people would be killed by the initial nuclear radiation of the bomb—the radiation delivered during the first minute after a detonation. Within an area four miles in diameter under the bomb, 50 percent of the people shielded by as much as two feet of concrete would be killed by the initial gamma rays and neutrons.

We may get a good idea of what would happen to the United States in a nuclear war from the testimony given before the Special Subcommittee on Radiation of the Joint Congressional Committee on Atomic Energy by Dr. William W. Kellogg and Mr. Charles Shafer. Dr. Kellogg is a physicist who is a research scientist with the Rand Corporation and Mr. Shafer is a meteorologist who had been transferred from the Weather Bureau to the Radiological Defense Operations Office of the Federal Civil Defense Administration.

They described in some detail the predicted effects of a hypothetical attack on the United States with thermonuclear weapons. It was assumed that 250 bombs would be dropped on 144 areas of attack. Fifty-three of the areas were basically population and industrial centers, 59 areas were basically military installations, and the remaining 32 areas contained both military and population objectives. The bombs were assumed to be superbombs with 5 megatons, 10 megatons, or 20 megatons energy, averaging 10 megatons, and totaling 2500 megatons.

It was pointed out by Mr. Shafer that it had not been assumed that 100 percent of the weapons would get through to the target. He said "We assumed that this represented those aircraft that were able to penetrate our borders and deliver their weapons. I do not know how many aircraft that would require. If the Air Defense Command were effective in knocking down 50 percent of the invading bomber aircraft, this would imply 500, perhaps, in the original attack."

He also said that attacks with much less and much greater megatonnage than this had been studied. He mentioned a study based upon the detonation of 20 megatons above each of 314 targets in the United States, a total of about 6000 megatons of explosives (this is about 2000 times the amount of explosive energy of all of the bombs used in the Second World War).

Dr. Joseph Rotblat, Professor of Physics in the Medical College in St. Bartholomew's Hospital in London, has suggested in an article in the January 1958 issue of the *Bulletin of the Atomic Scientists* that as much as 25,000 megatons of bombs might be used in an attack on the United States, because in an all-out war each side would aim at knocking out the enemy in the shortest possible time, so as to reduce the danger of retaliation. He pointed out that the number of bombs would be determined largely by the accumulated stockpile, and that the stockpiles may be very large a few years from now.

A nuclear war involving 10,000 megatons of weapons is one that might be contemplated in the immediate future. It is likely that the stockpiles of nuclear weapons are such as to permit such a war to be carried out, and that the studies reported by Dr. Kellogg and Mr. Shafer were made because of this possibility. The nuclear war fought with ten times as many bombs, as suggested by Dr. Rotblat, may be a reasonable one to anticipate at some time in the future, perhaps by 1965 or 1970.

THE NATURE OF NUCLEAR WAR

In *The New York Times* for 28 January 1958 it is said that on 16 April 1957, according to an Associated Press dispatch from Washington, Congressman James Van Zandt, a member of the Joint Congressional Committee on Atomic Energy, stated that the United States had stockpiled material for the manufacture of 35,000 atomic weapons and that the Soviet Union had an estimated stockpile of 10,000 such weapons.

The following table of the effect of an attack of 250 nuclear weapons, totaling 2500 megatons, on the United States was given by Dr. Kellogg in his report (*The Nature of Radioactive Fallout and Its Effects on Man*, page 118).

Table 5

Effect of Attack on the United States with Nuclear Bombs Totaling 2500 Megatons

(Total population that for 1950, 151 million)

	Dead	Injured	Uninjured
1st day	36,000,000	57,000,000	58,000,000
7th day	51,000,000	42,000,000	58,000,000
14th day	61,000,000	31,000,000	58,000,000
60th day	72,000,000	21,000,000	58,000,000

Dr. Kellogg made the following statement in his testimony: "Those dead on the first day were presumably killed by the immediate effects of the bombs, i.e., mostly blast and thermal effects. The subsequent rise in fatalities reflects the delayed effects of radiation damage, coupled in many cases to external injuries. While one should not take these actual numbers too literally, their orders of magnitude and the trends shown here are fairly realistic. In particular, the indication that fallout might account for a large number of deaths—nearly as many as died by the immediate effects—is pertinent. In actuality, many of the 'uninjured' ones would be caught by the fallout as they tried to move about. Clearly, however, such figures can only be illustrative, since the behavior patterns of the population would have a tremendous effect on the casualties due to radiation."

We may bring the table of casualties up to date by correcting from the 1950 population figures (151 million) to the estimated 175 million for 1958, obtaining the following table:

Table 6

Effect of Attack on the United States with Nuclear Bombs
Totaling 2500 Megatons
(Population 175,000,000 for 1958)

	Dead	Injured	Uninjured
1st day	42,000,000	66,000,000	67,000,000
7th day	59,000,000	49,000,000	67,000,000
14th day	71,000,000	37,000,000	67,000,000
60th day	83,000,000	25,000,000	67,000,000

In his testimony Mr. Shafer referred to a chart which has been reproduced and is given here as Figure 8. This chart shows the predicted conditions with respect to radioactive fallout. The black areas are areas in which the radioactivity is over 1000 roentgens per hour at a time one hour after the attack, and the dotted areas are areas in which the radioactivity is somewhere between 10 roentgens per hour and 1000 roentgens per hour one hour after the attack.

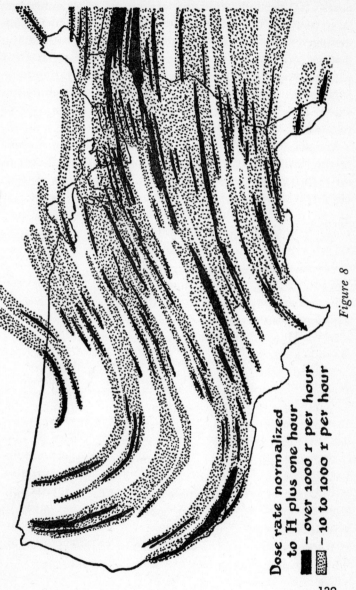

Figure 8

Dose rate normalized
to H plus one hour
■ – over 1000 r per hour
▦ – 10 to 1000 r per hour

Mr. Shafer said: "Without target evacuation, target area evacuation to escape primary weapons effects, and assuming present-day shielding which exists in the United States, that is, homes or home basements, or the basements of large administration buildings, the bomb damage assessment on this particular attack indicated a total loss by death of about 82 million people based upon current United States population, and about 24 million surviving casualties, 60 days subsequent to the attack. This left about 60 million relatively uninjured but doubtlessly suffering from radiation effects. In this particular analysis we only carried it down to the 10 roentgens per hour. So that even in the white areas where the levels are relatively low, there could be some radiation effect. Of the total fatalities, some 50 percent were a result of radiation factors."

He also made the following statements, in answer to questions: "Our computations went for the first 60 days. There may have been some deaths beyond then, because as pointed out yesterday, the delivery of radiation exceeds 60 days. However, certainly the bulk of the problem would be indicated.

"In this particular exercise, we dealt only with the immediate survival problem. We did not take into account the soil contamination, the uptake of strontium-90 and the long-term problem that certainly would be very much with us from an attack of this magnitude.

"No, we did not take contamination of water into account here. Certainly there would be considerable contamination of reservoirs from fallout, from rainfall, moving the deposition from its point of contact and into reservoirs."

Representative Holifield asked him if this represented the immediate effect, say, the within-24-hour effect. Mr.

Shafer answered as follows: "As far as this analysis of the fallout is concerned, yes. The mortality of fatality statistics which I gave you indicated the first sixty days. As far as contamination of water is concerned, certainly Southern Lake Michigan would have had a considerable amount of this. Many cities depend upon their drinking water from Lake Michigan."

This analysis of a hypothetical nuclear attack on the United States has led to the conclusion that over one half of the people in the United States would be dead at the end of sixty days after the attack, as a result of injuries received during the first 24 hours. The additional radiation effect during the period after 24 hours might be such as to cause the deaths of some additional millions or tens of millions. Moreover, as pointed out by Dr. Rotblat, the attack might be considerably heavier than the assumed 2500-megaton attack.

I conclude that, in contemplating a possible nuclear war, we should estimate that between one half and three quarters of the people in the United States would be dead at the end of sixty days.

Let us make an estimate for the world as a whole. Casualties might well be as great, proportionately, in the U.S.S.R., with 225 million people, in Europe as a whole, with 425 million, and in some of the adjacent regions in which there may be military bases. Altogether, about one billion people in the world might be in the regions in which there would be heavy nuclear attack. Between one half and three quarters of this total might be dead within sixty days after the attack—between 500 million and 750 million.

I can understand the basis for the testimony given by General Gavin before a Congressional Committee, that several hundred million, perhaps as many as 800 million, casualties would result from a nuclear war.

The Effect of Fallout

So far we have not taken into consideration the effect of fallout, except that of local fallout during the first 24 hours.

Let us make a calculation of the probable genetic and somatic effects of fallout from a nuclear war.

I assume as the basis of the first calculation that a nuclear war is fought in which the attack on the United States is the one discussed by Dr. Kellogg and Mr. Shafer, with 2500 megatons of bombs involved. I assume further that a similar quantity is detonated over Europe, aside from the U.S.S.R., and that twice the quantity, 5000 megatons, is detonated over the U.S.S.R. The total amount of nuclear explosives involved thus is assumed to be 10,000 megatons. I assume that the fission yield is 50 percent; that is, 5000 megatons of fission.

I shall also make a rough calculation on the basis of the assumption that ten times as much explosive is used; that is, 50,000 megatons of fission. This assumption corresponds to the suggestion by Dr. Rotblat that in the course of time stockpiles will become great enough to permit an attack ten times as great as the 2500-megaton attack on the United States.

Dr. Ralph E. Lapp, who, without access to any secret information, discovered that the 1 March 1954 Bikini bomb had a third fission stage of uranium-238 long before this information was released by the AEC, has assumed that superbombs might have a considerably larger fission stage than I have assumed, namely, as large as twice the fusion stage (*The Nature of Radioactive Fallout and Its Effects on Man*, page 1280). Accordingly the amount of radioactivity involved in a nuclear attack such as we are discussing might be considerably greater than in the estimates that I have made. An important factor is that it costs very little to obtain a great increase in explosive power and amount of radioactive fallout from a bomb by adding additional ordinary uranium to the third stage.

We cannot hope to make a precise estimate of the damage that would be done by fallout radioactivity, but we can get an idea of the order of magnitude by making several simple calculations. Let us begin by quoting again from the testimony of Dr. Alvin C. Graves before the Special Subcommittee on Radiation of the Joint Congressional Committee on Atomic Energy (*The Nature of Radioactive Fallout and Its Effects on Man*, page 58). Dr. Graves is a physicist who since 1950 has been Science Director of the Pacific Proving Ground Activities and since 1951 Test Director of the Nevada Proving Ground Activities of the Atomic Energy Commission. I judge that his statements about fallout are accurate.

In his testimony he said: "About 0.11 pounds of fission products are produced for each kiloton of fission energy yield and its radioactivity at one minute would be comparable with that of many pounds of radium. A megaton of fission energy would, therefore, result in activity at one minute comparable with that of very many tons of radium. During the first 24 hours there would be a decrease by a factor by more than 6000, but it has been estimated that this activity, if uniformly spread over 10,000 square miles, would cause a radiation intensity after 24 hours of 2.7 roentgens per hour at a distance of three feet above the ground. Unprotected personnel in that area would receive more than 300 roentgens after the first day. During the first day they would receive many times that amount."

We may use his statement that one megaton of fission gives radioactive fission products such that if spread uniformly over 10,000 square miles an exposure of 300 roentgens to unprotected personnel would be obtained after the first day.

Let us assume that the fission products are spread uniformly over the surface of the earth in the neighborhood of the explosions—this is the reason that Dr. Graves used the area 10,000 square miles as that over which to spread the fallout products of the bomb. The area of the United States is three million square miles and that of Europe and the parts of the U.S.S.R. that would be subjected to attack is somewhat over twice this amount, so that we may take ten million square miles as the area in which the bombs would fall.

Five thousand megatons of fission gives fission products which if spread uniformly over the area of ten million square miles would produce an exposure to unprotected personnel of 1500 roentgens during the period beginning 24 hours after the attack, and much more before that time.

The large attack, with 50,000 megatons of fission, would produce 15,000 roentgens exposure to unprotected personnel after the first 24 hours.

The evidence that exposure of human beings to large amounts of radiation, of this order of magnitude, causes a decrease in life expectancy of approximately five to ten days per roentgen is so strong that we have to accept this as a fact. An exposure of 1500 roentgens means, then, a decrease in life expectancy of 20 years to 40 years. This exposure has to be considered almost a lethal exposure, an

144

exposure that causes death, either immediately or within a few years.

How many people would receive this much exposure from a standard nuclear attack? People would, of course, avoid the radioactive regions and attempt to protect themselves. Moreover, the radioactivity would be concentrated in the regions of the attacks—roughly in the regions represented in Figure 8 by the black areas and the dotted areas and in contiguous regions, if the distribution of bombs is as assumed in this study. In these regions the amount of radioactivity would be much greater than in the white regions.

But it is just in these regions where the attacks would be made that the major part of the people of the United States live.

I think that we have to conclude that the testimony elicited from Dr. Kellogg and Mr. Shafer was incomplete. They testified that in a population of 175 million subjected to a standard attack involving 2500 megatons of bombs with high fission yield, 108 million would be dead after 60 days as a result of the blast, fire, and radiation effects of the first 24 hours. Our calculation, just above, of the radiation effects after the first 24 hours suggests strongly that a large fraction of the 67 million survivors would also die from the later effects of the local fallout radioactivity.

If the attack were to be ten times greater, the average exposure of unprotected personnel from fallout radioactivity after 24 hours would be 15,000 roentgens, assuming equal distribution of the fission products over the whole of the area of the United States. This amount of radioactivity is so great that it is hard to see how anyone could remain living for long in the general regions of the

145

attack. Only the people in isolated regions, where no bombs were dropped, could hope to survive such a great nuclear war.

Nuclear War and Strontium-90

The major part of the fission products of a nuclear explosion falls to earth in the local fallout, in case that the explosion is a surface explosion, with the fireball touching the surface of the earth. These explosions are more effective militarily than explosions high in the atmosphere, for several reasons, and the foregoing analysis of a hypothetical nuclear attack on the United States was carried out with the assumption that the explosions were all surface explosions.

As much as 80 percent of the radioactive fallout products may be contained within the local fallout. The remainder, constituting the worldwide fallout, is distributed more or less uniformly over the surface of the earth. It is the cesium-137 and strontium-90 that need to be given special attention in the worldwide fallout.

The standard nuclear attack that we have been discussing would produce about 100 times as much worldwide fallout as will be produced by all of the bomb tests that have been made so far (to 1958). The still greater nuclear war that we foresee as a possibility for ten years in the future would produce 1000 times as much worldwide fallout as the tests that have been made so far.

The studies of Dr. J. Laurence Kulp and his associates at Columbia University on the amount of strontium-90 in bones have led him to conclude that a probable level of strontium-90 in the bones of human beings as a result of the tests already made will be 2.9 micromicrocuries per gram of calcium by 1977, when much of the strontium-90 that is now in the stratosphere has descended to the surface of the earth.

Accordingly the value to be expected as a result of a standard nuclear war is 290 micromicrocuries of strontium-90 per gram of calcium. The value to be expected as a result of the still greater nuclear war of ten years from now is 2900 micromicrocuries of strontium-90 per gram of calcium.

If these values were reached there would be a considerable amount of damage done to the health of human beings. On the basis of our assumption about the dependence of incidence of leukemia and bone cancer on amount of radiation exposure, we may estimate that some millions of such cases of these diseases would be caused among the two billion survivors of the nuclear war. These additional cases of leukemia and bone cancer would, however, be distributed over a number of years, and the military leaders of nations might feel that the sacrifice of some of their own people to an effective attack on the enemy was justified.

Nuclear War and the Human Race

The genetic consequences of a nuclear war would be terribly serious—100 times or 1000 times as serious as the effects of the bomb tests that have been carried out.

We may estimate from the exposures of the gonads to fallout radiation from the bomb tests that the gonad exposure during the first thirty years of life of children and young people during the 30-year period following a standard nuclear war, with 5000 megatons of fission, would amount to somewhere between 10 roentgens and 50 roentgens. This is in the range of the estimates of the doubling dose of the mutation rate by radiation, and accordingly the mutation rate would be doubled for that generation. A smaller effect would be found in each succeeding generation, as the amount of radioactivity decreased.

The mutation rate for human beings all over the world would be increased by approximately ten-fold by the worldwide fallout from a still greater nuclear war, with 50,000 megatons of fission.

In addition, consideration must be given to the genetic effects of the local fallout in the countries where the nuclear bombs were exploded. With possible exposures of the magnitudes of thousands of roentgens, the genetic effects would be expected to be very great in these countries. Many people would be rendered sterile. Many would have seriously defective children. There would also be some populations, in regions far distant from the places where bomb tests were carried out, where the genetic effect was small, and there might be a great effort in the post-nuclear-war period for these populations to preserve the integrity of their pool of germ plasm and to remain isolated from the mutated populations in the surrounding regions.

The people in India, China, Africa, South America, and Australia would also be affected by the radiation from the worldwide fallout. For them the number of seriously defective children born might increase from its present value of 2 percent to a considerably larger value, and in addition there would be a corresponding increase in the number of mutant genes producing smaller disabilities. Dr. H. J. Muller in his address "The Radiation Danger," published in the *Colorado Quarterly* for 1958, has pointed out that the total load of mutant genes in the population at the present time is such that about one person in five dies without progeny because of their effect, and hence if the

148

load were to be increased five-fold there might be serious consequences.

There is a real possibility that a great nuclear war would change the nature of the pool of human germ plasm in such a way that the human species, as we know it, would not survive. This danger is a significant one for people living in every part of the world, but especially great for those in countries in which the nuclear war would be fought.

The "Clean" Bomb

Ever since the possibility of making a hydrogen bomb was first discussed it has been recognized that nuclear bombs could be made with either a larger amount or a smaller amount of radioactive products.

The bomb of the Hiroshima type or the Nagasaki type produces a weight of radioactive fission products approximately equal to the weight of uranium-235 or plutonium-239 that has undergone fission. Also, a weight of radioactive fission products is produced approximately equal to that of the uranium that undergoes fission during the third stage of the detonation of a fission-fusion-fission superbomb, in addition to the products from the first fission stage. On the other hand, the fusion stage of a hydrogen bomb or a superbomb does not produce any very large quantity of radioactive products under ordinary conditions, except carbon-14.

A 20-megaton superbomb might produce the radioactive fission products corresponding to 10 megatons of fission, whereas a 20-megaton hydrogen bomb might produce radioactive materials corresponding in the main only to the 40 kilotons of fission involved in its first stage. For the same explosive power, the hydrogen bomb would have

149

produced only 4 percent as much radioactive material other than carbon-14 as the superbomb.

The superbomb is called a "dirty" bomb and the hydrogen bomb a "clean" bomb. This is the basis of the statement made by President Eisenhower that a 96-percent clean bomb had been made.

There is, of course, the possibility that a bomb with still smaller ratio of radioactive products to explosive power can be constructed. Atomic bombs (fission bombs) with as small as 1 kiloton energy have been detonated. I do not know whether or not they contained a larger amount of fissionable material than the amount that underwent fission, but there is the possibility that the small amount of uranium-235 or plutonium-239 that would give 1 kiloton equivalent of explosive energy could be made to undergo essentially complete fission. If, then, a hydrogen bomb could be designed in such a way that this small amount of fissionable material would cause the fusion stage to take place, such a bomb, with total explosive power of 20 megatons, could be described as 99.9-percent clean (except for its carbon-14).

There are probably some serious technical difficulties involved in making a bomb with as little radioactivity as this, but there is a possibility that it can be done.

It is, on the other hand, unlikely that a bomb can be constructed in the near future that involves no fission whatever. Moreover, in order that there be no radioactivity, no materials could be used in the construction of the bomb itself that could absorb neutrons to produce radioactivity isotopes, and no air could be around when it explodes.

In several speeches I have objected to the use of the expression the "clean" bomb. I have said that to call any weapon that can kill millions of people a "clean" bomb is to insult a noble word in the English language—the word clean. This comment, of course, has nothing to do with the radioactivity of the fission products; it is the expression of an objection to the immorality of war, and especially of nuclear war.

The argument has been used by President Eisenhower and by Dr. Teller that it is essential that the testing of nuclear weapons be continued in order that clean bombs be developed. For example, Drs. Teller and Latter in their article in *Life* Magazine said: "If we stop testing now and if we should fail to develop to the fullest possible extent these clean weapons, we would unnecessarily kill a great number of noncombatants in a future war. Not to develop the explosives with the smallest possible radioactive fallout would, indeed, be completely inexcusable."

I believe that the argument is fallacious. It seems to suggest that nuclear wars might be fought with non-radioactive weapons only.

Drs. Teller and Latter say that the fallout radioactivity might kill people in our own country or in the country whose liberty we are trying to defend and that we should for this reason be able to use nuclear weapons that cause the least possible contamination. They do not say that we should use nuclear weapons with little radioactivity in attacking the enemy country, and, in fact, we may be sure that in a nuclear war the weapons that would be used in attacking the enemy country, and that would be used against us, would be weapons with a large amount of radioactive fallout.

War is conducted in such a way as to produce the greatest damage to the enemy. A military leader who is given a choice between the principles of humanity and an effective defense of his nation always abandons the principles of humanity.

During the Second World War it was found that the saturation bombing of cities, doing damage to women and children and other non-combatants, was a far more effective way of waging war than the bombing of military objectives only, and the saturation way, despite its greater immorality, was adopted.

Far greater damage can be done to an enemy nation with the use of superbombs than can be done, for the same amount of effort, with the use of hydrogen bombs.

Let us, for example, assume that we have a stockpile of some thousands of 10-megaton superbombs. Each of them may have, as part of its design, a tamper in the form of a metal shell surrounding the fusionable material. If this tamper, perhaps a one-thousand-pound metal shell, is replaced by a similar one-thousand-pound shell made of the metal uranium, the bomb is converted from a 10-megaton hydrogen bomb to a 20-megaton superbomb. The cost of this conversion is practically zero—perhaps $15,000 for the uranium. For this small cost the bomb is changed into a superbomb with twice the explosive power and nearly twice the power of causing destruction and death through blast, fire, and immediate radiation effects. And, moreover, it is changed from a bomb with little radioactivity to a bomb with great radioactivity. The superbomb, detonated near the ground, can discharge as much as 80 percent of its radioactive fission products into a radioactive local fallout that in large part descends within an hour or two over an area of 10,000 square miles near the point of explosion, with the possibility of killing through its radioactivity a large fraction of the people in this area of 10,000 square miles. This makes the weapon such a powerful one, in comparison with the 10-megaton hydrogen bomb, that no military leader would be willing to forego its use.

Moreover, there is little reason to expect that he would be dissuaded from using the weapon by the damage that the radioactivity would do to his own countrymen. Only 20 percent of the fission products would go into the atmosphere, to descend later on, over a period of years, as worldwide fallout. A large fraction of the radioactive material would have decomposed before descending to the surface of the earth, and the effects of the remaining radioactive material may be described, as has been done so often by representatives of the AEC in discussing the tests, as being "negligible" or as being "small in comparison with many risks that we take in our everyday life."

There is no hope that a nuclear war will be fought with "clean" bombs. The "clean" bomb, in fact, may be a red herring which causes people to cease to worry about the perils of radioactivity. In the summer of 1957 it seemed to serve effectively as propaganda to stop, for a while, the growing concern about the horrors of nuclear weapons and nuclear war.

We might ask the question "Would it not be possible to achieve an international agreement to use only 'clean' bombs in future wars?" This is, however, not a sensible question. If such an international agreement could be reached, under which the great nations of the world would agree to limit themselves in a really serious way in waging war, it should be possible to reach international agreements about disputed questions without resorting to war at all.

If our nuclear future includes nuclear war, the world is lost.

The Cobalt Bomb

A few years ago Dr. James R. Arnold of the University of Chicago published an article in the *Bulletin of the Atomic Scientists* about the possibility of wiping out all life on earth with the use of the cobalt bomb. He reached the conclusion that it would be possible, for a few billion dollars invested in hydrogen bombs with shells of the metal cobalt about them, to do the job.

The cobalt bomb is a hydrogen bomb or superbomb with a shell of perhaps 1000 pounds of the common metal cobalt about it. Cobalt, as found in nature, consists entirely of the stable isotope cobalt-59. The nuclei of the cobalt-59 atoms absorb neutrons, changing into cobalt-60. Cobalt-60 is a radioactive nucleus. It has a half-life of five years, and it emits gamma rays which have large penetrating power, so that they can do much damage to human beings.

A cobalt bomb presumably could be made in such a way that, for a surface explosion, over 80 percent of the radioactive materials would be deposited as local fallout within a few hundred miles of the place of explosion of the bomb. Possibly the bomb could be constructed so that 90 percent or more would be deposited as local fallout. With its half-life of five years the cobalt-60 would contaminate the region for long periods of time, half of it remaining after five years, one quarter of it after ten years. The gamma rays that it produces can penetrate a foot or more of concrete.

I do not know just how great an amount of radioactivity could be produced in this way by a superbomb converted into a cobalt bomb, but I estimate that the radioactivity of the fallout might be increased in its effectiveness a

154

hundred-fold over that of an ordinary superbomb. There is a possibility that the cobalt bomb could be used as an important offensive weapon, such that the military leaders would be assured that by the use of some hundreds of these bombs everyone in the enemy country would be killed.

No cobalt bomb has been tested. There is no need to test it, because its structure is so simple and the principles involved are so well understood that there is certainty about its performance, even without a test.

It may be that there are cobalt bombs stored in the stockpiles of thousands of nuclear weapons in the U.S.S.R. and the United States, perhaps even in some of the military bases in other countries, where great bombing planes circle about with their loads of nuclear weapons.

Dr. Teller and Dr. Latter, in a chapter on the cobalt bomb in their book *Our Nuclear Future,* say that "The question of the cobalt bomb or radiological warfare in general is not whether it is feasible—it is—but rather whether it serves a useful military purpose." Then they point out that "It is not impossible that situations might arise in which radiological warfare could be militarily advantageous."

They mention that, instead of cobalt, other materials might be introduced into a nuclear weapon, so that other radioactive substances would be produced by absorption of neutrons by their nuclei. They mention that the bomb might be constructed in such a way that almost all of the radioactivity would be precipitated near the explosion, so that distant localities would not be seriously affected, and they say that "It is conceivable, therefore, that radiological warfare could be used in a humane manner."

I judge that the last statement is to be taken to mean

that radiological warfare might conceivably be used in a manner less inhumane than other types of nuclear warfare. I fear, however, that only on rare occasions would the less inhumane ways of waging nuclear war be also the most effective, and that there is no hope for the world if our future is one of nuclear warfare. I fear that a great nuclear war would mean the end of this beautiful world in which we live, the end of civilization.

8
The Scientists
Appeal for Peace

Many statements about nuclear weapons and war have been made by scientists since the nuclear age began.

Even before the first nuclear bomb had been tested it became clear to the scientists working on the project that the new weapons were a herald of man's mastery of an entirely new world of overwhelming forces, and that a new kind of statesmanship would be needed to steer mankind away from disaster.

A memorandum directed to President Roosevelt was written by Dr. Leo Szilard in March 1945. In this memorandum it was pointed out that a system of international control of nuclear weapons might give us a chance of living through this century without having our cities destroyed. President Roosevelt died before this memorandum reached him. On 28 May 1945, six weeks before the first bomb was tested in New Mexico, Dr. Szilard discussed this memorandum in a personal interview with Mr. James F. Byrnes, to whom it had been referred by the White House. The full text of the Szilard Memorandum has not yet been published; excerpts were printed in the December 1947 issue of the *Bulletin of the Atomic Scientists*.

A report on "Social and Political Implications of Atomic

157

Energy," called the Franck Report, was transmitted to the Secretary of War on 11 June 1945. It had been prepared by a committee of three physicists, three chemists, and one biologist: Drs. James Franck (chairman), Donald Hughes, Leo Szilard, Thorfin Hogness, Glenn Seaborg, Eugene Rabinowitch, and J. J. Nickson. Its primary purpose was to warn against the use of the atomic bomb against Japan. It contained the statements "We believe that these considerations make the use of nuclear bombs for an early unannounced attack against Japan inadvisable. If the United States were to be the first to release this new means of indiscriminate destruction on mankind, she would sacrifice public support throughout the world, precipitate the race for armaments, and prejudice the possibility of reaching an international agreement on the future control of such weapons."

The Franck Report was published in the *Bulletin of the Atomic Scientists* on 1 May 1946.

Since 1945 there have been many appeals by scientists and by laymen for sanity in the nuclear world—so many that they cannot all be reproduced here. The texts of a few of them are given as appendixes to this book, beginning with a statement made by Albert Einstein in 1946 (Appendix 1).

On 15 July 1955 a declaration was issued calling on all nations to renounce force as a final resort of policy. This declaration, with the names of the 52 Nobel Laureates who signed it, is given in Appendix 2.

At the same time, July 1955, the Russell-Einstein appeal was issued. This appeal, which was formulated by Bertrand Russell and was signed by Einstein a few days before his death, pointed out the dangers of thermonuclear weapons. It contained the statement "There lies before us, if we choose, continual progress in happiness, knowledge and wisdom. Shall we, instead, choose death, because we cannot forget our quarrels? We appeal, as human beings, to human beings: remember your humanity and forget the rest. If you can do so, the way lies open to a new paradise; if you cannot, there lies before you the risk of universal death."

The signers of the appeal (Max Born, P. W. Bridgman, Albert Einstein, L. Infeld, F. Joliot-Curie, H. J. Muller, Linus Pauling, C. F. Powell, J. Rotblat, Bertrand Russell, and Hideki Yukawa) asked that an international congress of scientists be convened, and urged that they pass the following resolution: "In view of the fact that in any future world war nuclear weapons will certainly be employed, and that such weapons threaten the continued existence of mankind, we urge the Governments of the world to realize, and to acknowledge publicly, that their purposes cannot be furthered by a world war, and we urge them, consequently, to find peaceful means for the settlement of all matters of dispute between them."

In response to this appeal a conference (the First Pugwash Conference) was held in Pugwash, Nova Scotia, in July 1957. A stirring and informative report was prepared, and it was signed by twenty scientists, of ten nations. The report covered the hazards arising from the use of atomic energy in peace and war, the problem of the control of nuclear weapons, and the social responsibility of scientists.

Three Soviet scientists were among those at Pugwash. On their return to Moscow they made a report to the Academy of Sciences of the U.S.S.R., and they prepared a statement supporting the Pugwash report, ending with the sentence: "We Soviet scientists express our full readiness for common effort with scientists of any other country, to discuss any proposals directed toward the prevention of atomic war and the creation of secure peace and tranquility for all mankind." This statement was signed by 198 members of the Academy of Sciences and other Soviet academies.

The Second Pugwash Conference was held in April 1958, and plans were made for a larger one to be held in September 1958.

Among other appeals by scientists, that of 13 April 1957 signed by 18 leading physicists of West Germany is noteworthy in that these scientists not only urged West Germany to renounce nuclear weapons of all kinds, but also stated that they would not take part in the production, testing, or use of nuclear weapons.

On 24 April 1957 the Declaration of Conscience by Dr. Albert Schweitzer was broadcast from Oslo. This great document is reproduced as Appendix 3.

The Scientists' Petition to the United Nations

At noon on Monday 15 January 1958 I placed in the hands of Mr. Dag Hammarskjold, Secretary-General of the United Nations, a petition from 9235 scientists, of many countries in the world.

This petition has the title "Petition to the United Nations Urging that an International Agreement to Stop the Testing of Nuclear Bombs be Made Now."

The petition consists of five paragraphs, as follows:

We, the scientists whose names are signed below, urge that an international agreement to stop the testing of nuclear bombs be made now.

Each nuclear bomb test spreads an added burden of

radioactive elements over every part of the world. Each added amount of radiation causes damage to the health of human beings all over the world and causes damage to the pool of human germ plasm such as to lead to an increase in the number of seriously defective children that will be born in future generations.

So long as these weapons are in the hands of only three powers an agreement for their control is feasible. If testing continues, and the possession of these weapons spreads to additional governments, the danger of outbreak of a cataclysmic nuclear war through the reckless action of some irresponsible national leader will be greatly increased.

An international agreement to stop the testing of nuclear bombs now could serve as a first step toward a more general disarmament and the ultimate effective abolition of nuclear weapons, averting the possibility of a nuclear war that would be a catastrophe to all humanity.

We have in common with our fellow men a deep concern for the welfare of all human beings. As scientists we have knowledge of the dangers involved and therefore a special responsibility to make those dangers known. We deem it imperative that immediate action be taken to effect an international agreement to stop the testing of all nuclear weapons.

The letter that was given to Mr. Hammarskjold together with the petition and the names of the 9235 scientists reads as follows:

Sir:

On behalf of 9235 scientists of many countries of the world, I submit herewith the accompanying petition urging that an international agreement to stop the testing of nuclear bombs be made now, as a first step toward a more general disarmament.

The petition is submitted by my 9234 fellow scientists and me as individuals. No organization has been responsible for the planning or writing of the petition or for the collection of signatures.

The petition resulted from an address on Science in the Modern World given by me in the Chapel of Washington University, St. Louis, Missouri, to the students and faculty of the University on May 15, 1957. The response to this address was so enthusiastic as to suggest that a statement be prepared to which American scientists could subscribe. I wrote the statement, which is the accompanying petition, on that day, and within a few days twenty-six other U.S. scientists had signed: Barry Commoner, Edward U. Condon, Charles D. Coryell, Leslie C. Dunn, Viktor Hamburger, Michael Heidelberger, I. H. Herskowitz, Herbert Jehle, Martin Kamen, Edwin C. Kemble, I. M. Kolthoff, Chauncey Leake, S. E. Luria, Max Mason, Carl V. Moore, Philip Morrison, Hermann J. Muller, Severo Ochoa, C. C. Price, Arthur Roberts, M. L. Sands, Verner Schomaker, Laurence H. Snyder, Oswald Veblen, M. B. Visscher, W. H. Zachariasen. Within two weeks the signatures of over 2000 U.S. scientists had been obtained, and on the fourth of June 1957 I submitted the statement to the President of the United States of America.

In July 1957 I received a voluntary statement of adherence to the petition from all of the professors of science (forty in number) of the Free University of Brussels, and similar statements from scientists in several other countries. I later wrote to a few scientists in every country, asking that they sign the petition and obtain other signatures.

So far the petition has been signed by 9235 scientists, of 44 countries. Among the signers are 36 Nobel Laureates, representing 12 countries. Their names are given in the first list (and repeated in the main list). Separate lists are also given of 101 members of the Academy of Sciences of the United States of America, 35 Fellows of the Royal Society of London, England, and 216 Members and Correspondents of the Academy of Sciences of the U.S.S.R.

In some countries only a few distinguished scientists have signed the petition; an example is Sweden, with two signers, both Nobel Laureates. In others (Japan, Rumania) the effort seems to have been made by my correspondents to request nearly all of the scientists of the nation to sign. Sir C. V. Raman, of India, a Nobel Laureate in physics, wrote that in his opinion every scientist in India would sign the petition if he had the opportunity; the number of Indian signers, 535, should not be taken to mean that many scientists are opposed. It is my opinion that the petition represents the feelings of the great majority of the scientists of the world.

We urge that an international agreement to stop the testing of nuclear weapons be made now. The details of the agreement should, of course, be such that it be effective, and that, so far as possible, it benefit all nations and all people equally, not one nation or group of nations preferentially. We urge that this agreement be made as a first step toward a more general disarmament, and we hope that later steps will be taken without delay.

It is not my belief that this problem is one that should

163

be settled by scientists; it is instead one of importance to every person in the world. My colleagues and I feel, however, that it is worth while for us to express our opinion to you, as we have done with this petition, inasmuch as it is the scientists who have some measure of understanding of the complex factors involved in the problem, such as the magnitude of the genetic and somatic effects of the released radioactive materials. This may be illustrated by the statement of one of the signers of the petition, J. H. Burn, F.R.S., Professor of Pharmacology in the University of Oxford, that "We are particularly concerned about the role of uptake in the bones of children of radioactive strontium from the milk they drink."

We are also, of course, greatly concerned about the danger of outbreak of a cataclysmic war. We believe that international problems should be solved not by war, but by the application of man's power to reason—through arbitration, negotiation, international agreements, international law—and that a just and effective international agreement to stop bomb tests would be a good first step.

Respectfully yours,

LINUS PAULING

It is mentioned in the letter that there were 36 Nobel Laureates among the signers. The signature of one additional Nobel Laureate was added to the list later. These 37 Nobel Laureates, of thirteen countries, are all scientists, although two of them, Albert Schweitzer and Lord Boyd Orr, received their Nobel prizes in peace, and one, Bertrand Russell, received his in literature. Of the others, nine received Nobel prizes in physics, twelve in chemistry, and thirteen in physiology and medicine.

Eight of the Nobel Laureates are Americans, seven are British, eight are German, two are French, two are Chinese (both residing now in the United States, where they made the discovery that led to the award of the Nobel prize to them), two are Swedish, two Swiss, one Irish, one Japanese, one Indian, one Hungarian (now resident in the United States), one Belgian, and one Russian.

The names of the Nobel Laureates who signed the petition are given in the following list:

Nobel Laureates Among Signers

Nobel Laureates in Physics

Max Born
  Germany

P. A. M. Dirac
  Great Britain

W. Heisenberg
  Germany

Tang-Dao Lee
  (Resident in U.S.A.)
  China

E. T. S. Walton
  Ireland

C. F. Powell
  Great Britain

C. V. Raman
  India

C. N. Yang
  (Resident in U.S.A.)
  China

Hideki Yukawa
  Japan

Nobel Laureates in Chemistry

K. Alder
  Germany

A. Butenandt
  Germany

Otto Hahn
  Germany

Frederic Joliot-Curie
  France

Richard Kuhn
  Germany

Linus Pauling
  U.S.A.

Leopold Ruzicka	A. W. K. Tiselius
Switzerland	Sweden
N. N. Semenov	Harold Urey
U.S.S.R.	U.S.A.
R. L. M. Synge	Adolf Windaus
Great Britain	Germany

Nobel Laureate in Literature

Bertrand Russell
  Great Britain

Nobel Laureates in Peace

| Lord Boyd Orr | Albert Schweitzer |
| Great Britain | France |

Nobel Laureates in Physiology and Medicine

Jules Bordet	W. P. Murphy
Belgium	U.S.A.
Henry Dale	A. Szent-Györgyi
Great Britain	(Resident in U.S.A.)
Gerhard Domagk	Hungary
Germany	Max Theiler
Joseph Erlanger	U.S.A.
U.S.A.	Hugo Theorell
Hans Krebs	Sweden
Great Britain	T. Reichstein
Otto Loewi	Switzerland
U.S.A.	G. H. Whipple
Hermann Muller	U.S.A.
U.S.A.	

Copies of the petition and of a list of names of some of the signers were delivered to all of the 82 national missions to the United Nations on the same day on which the petition was submitted.

I asked the Permanent Mission of India to the United Nations to circulate the petition, for they had repeatedly spoken out against nuclear tests since 1954. However, while they were waiting for their government's permission, the U.S.S.R. delegation, without consulting me and probably without knowing of India's interest in the petition, made a formal request of the Secretary-General that they be allowed to circulate the petition, and they did so on 28 February 1958.

In the meantime, many additional signatures had arrived in Pasadena, and a second list of names of scientists who had signed the petition brought the total number of scientists signing the petition to 11,021, representing 49 countries.

The petition was the result of the efforts of individual scientists. No organization was responsible for circulating the petition and gathering signatures. The whole job was done by a rather few people, and the entire expense, which was not very great, was borne by a few individuals, all scientists, except some volunteers who contributed some secretarial labor and one Pasadena resident who sent me a check for $100 to help defray the expenses.

I think that the ease with which the many thousands of signatures were obtained reflects the strong desire of scientists all over the world to contribute something to the solution of the urgent and all-important world problem that has been posed by the testing and stockpiling of the immense stores of nuclear weapons.

NO MORE WAR!

The Origin of the Appeal by American Scientists

For many years I have been concerned about the contradiction that exists between the ethical principles of behavior that apply to individual human beings, and are in general conformed to, and the immorality of the actions of nations and of national leaders, who are willing, instead of settling their differences in a moral and peaceful way, to sacrifice the lives of millions of human beings.

When I first heard that atomic bombs had been exploded over Hiroshima and Nagasaki in 1945 I was shocked, as were many other scientists, by the terrible powers of destruction that had been made available to man by the progress of science. Like many other scientists, I began to talk to groups of people—to luncheon clubs, to labor unions, to groups of students, to peace meetings— about the catastrophe that would come to the world if there were to be a war in which atomic bombs were used. Many times since 1945 I have talked to such groups about the overwhelming importance to the world of preserving peace.

On 26 March 1957 I spoke at the Santa Barbara Conference on World Affairs about the great problem that the world now faces, the problem of averting a nuclear war fought with hydrogen bombs and superbombs. It seemed to me that the citizens of Santa Barbara and the other participants in this Conference were more keenly aware than before of the possibility of a world catastrophe, but that there was considerable confusion and uncertainty in their minds as to the opinions of scientists, because of the apparent conflict between statements that had been published by scientists of the Atomic Energy Commission, and some others personally connected with the war effort, and those made by other scientists.

In his powerful radio address "A Declaration of Conscience," broadcast on 23 April 1957 from Oslo to most of the countries of the world, Dr. Albert Schweitzer pointed out that fallout radioactivity from the tests of great nuclear weapons causes damage to the health of human beings now living and to our descendants (Appendix 3). He called for an expression of informed public opinion in all nations that would lead the statesmen to reach an agreement to stop the bomb tests, and concluded by saying that "The end of further experiments with atom bombs would be like the early sunrays of hope which suffering humanity is longing for."

To this appeal by the great humanitarian, an answer was at once sent by AEC Commissioner Dr. Willard F. Libby. The answer contains statements that seem to be worded in such a way as to suggest to the reader that fallout does not cause damage: ". . . exposures from fallout are very much smaller than those which would be required to produce observable effects in the population." It contains no estimate of the number of people in the world who would be affected by fallout radioactivity, such as a scientist with more facts about the matter at his disposal than any other scientist in the world would be expected to make, but only reassurances and vague mention of extremely small risks, undetectable effects, hazards very much less than those that persons take as a normal part of their lives. This answer to Dr. Schweitzer and other statements made by Dr. Libby seemed to me to indicate that the AEC was not willing to trust the public with the facts of the true hazard.

Then on 15 May 1957 I spoke on the campus of Washington University in St. Louis. I had been invited by the faculty committee in charge to give an address in the Graham Memorial Chapel of the University on the occasion of the Eliot Honors Day Assembly, held in honor of the students who had been elected to Phi Beta Kappa, Sigma Xi, Order of the Coif, and other honor societies. The subject of my address was Science and the Modern World. I talked about how many wonderful aspects of the world had been found through the investigations of scientists. I talked about the discoveries of physicists—about electrons, the nuclei of atoms, protons, neutrons, neutrinos and antineutrinos; and also about the structure of molecules, about the way in which some human beings manufacture abnormal molecules of hemoglobin, which causes them to have a disease, a kind of hereditary hemolytic anemia. They manufacture these abnormal molecules because they have inherited bad genes from both father and mother. I mentioned that another bad gene, the gene for phenylketonuria, causes one percent of the cases of mental deficiency that are found in our mental hospitals. I mentioned that the bomb tests now being made are increasing the number of bad genes, and are probably also causing people to die of leukemia and other diseases. Then I said that Dr. Albert Schweitzer has said that "A humanitarian is a man who believes that no human being should be sacrificed to a project." I continued in the following way: "I am a humanitarian. I believe that no human being should be sacrificed to a project; and in particular I believe that no human being should be sacrificed to the project of perfecting nuclear weapons that could kill hundreds of millions of human beings, could devastate this beautiful world in which we live." I ended my address with a quotation from a letter written in 1780 by Benjamin Franklin to the scientist Joseph Priestley: "The rapid progress true Science now makes occasions my regretting sometimes that I was born so soon. It is impossible to imagine the height to which may be carried, in a thousand years, the power of man over matter. O that *Moral* science were in as fair a way of improvement, that men would cease to be wolves to one another, and that human beings would at length learn what they now improperly call *humanity.*"

The applause that came at the end of this address and the many questions as to whether there were some action that they could take that were asked me by some of the thousand students and members of the faculty of Washington University who were present made me decide to go ahead with the idea of preparing an appeal that could be signed by American scientists. This idea had arisen in a discussion that I had had the day before when I was telling Dr. Barry Commoner, Professor of Botany in Washington University and chairman of the committee that had invited me to give the Chapel address, what I planned to say in my address.

The Appeal by American Scientists

That afternoon I wrote the appeal, with the help of some of the Washington University scientists. Its wording was exactly the same as that of the petition to the United Nations, given earlier in this chapter, except that it began "We, the American scientists whose names are signed below . . ." Its heading was "An Appeal by American Scientists to the Governments and People of the World."

That evening some copies of the appeal were mimeographed and some letters were typed, which I sent to a few other scientists, asking if they would join me in making

171

the appeal. Within a week I had received answers from 26 of them; their names are listed in the letter to Mr. Hammarskjold that has been reproduced above.

On 22 May a few hundred copies of the appeal were printed and mailed to people in various universities and scientific laboratories in the United States. By ten days later, 2 June, the signatures of 2000 American scientists had reached me at my home in Pasadena. Many of the copies of the appeal that were returned have ten or twenty or thirty signatures attached.

It is significant that most of the leading geneticists of the country signed the appeal. It is, of course, the geneticists who understand best the damage that radiation can do to the human race by its action on the genes, and who are most concerned about this aspect of the bomb tests and of nuclear war.

On 3 June 1957 a statement about the Appeal by American Scientists was made to the press. A copy of the appeal, with a statement about it and the names of many of the signers, was also sent to the Special Subcommittee on Radiation of the Joint Committee on Atomic Energy of the Congress of the United States, which was holding hearings at that time. A letter and a copy of the Appeal were also sent to President Eisenhower.

Public mention of the Appeal by American Scientists was made by President Eisenhower in his press conference of 6 June 1957. When he was asked about his comment by Mr. James Reston of *The New York Times,* the President replied, "I said that there does seem to be some organization behind it [the Appeal by American Scientists]. I didn't say a wicked organization."

However, the President was mistaken in his surmise. The Appeal by American Scientists did not have any organization behind it; it was purely the result of private initiative and private enterprise on the part of individual scientists.

I believe that the Appeal by American Scientists in June 1957 did much good for the United States, in helping to correct some mistaken ideas about the United States and about American scientists that seem to have gained credence in foreign countries. From 9 June until 1 September 1957 my wife and I were in Europe, where we attended scientific congresses in several countries. Several scientists in these countries mentioned to us that the Appeal by American Scientists showed that American scientists are as concerned as those of other countries about the great problem of nuclear war and the related problem of the nuclear bomb tests.

The Origin of the Petition to the United Nations

The Appeal by American Scientists grew into the petition by scientists to the United Nations in a gradual and unexpected way.

On 8 June 1957, a few days after public announcement had been made about the Appeal by American Scientists, I was asked by a reporter in New York if scientists of other countries might join the appeal. I said "I should like to see the signatures of thousands of Russian scientists, of British and French scientists, of scientists of all countries of the world, to this appeal," and this statement was published in some newspapers.

A month later I received the following communication from the professors of science in the Free University of Brussels:

173

We, the undersigned members of the staff of the Free University of Brussels, associate ourselves with the Appeal by Professor Pauling and other American scientists urging that an international agreement be made now to stop the testing of all nuclear weapons.

It bore the signatures of 40 Belgian scientists.

Shortly thereafter several similar communications reached me from individual scientists and small groups of scientists in other countries, and on my return to Pasadena in September I decided that it would be worth while to ask scientists in other nations of the world to associate themselves with the Appeal by American Scientists. I employed a personal secretary for this purpose, and wrote about 500 letters to scientists in foreign countries. Many of these letters were to scientists whom I had met in international scientific meetings or on visits to foreign countries, or who had visited the California Institute of Technology in Pasadena. Others were addressed to scientists whose names were known to me because of their authorship of scientific papers. Other names were selected from reference books, especially the book *The World of Learning*, which lists all of the professors in the universities and learned institutions in the world.

These 500 letters were well received; they resulted in my getting about 7500 signatures of scientists in countries other than the United States.

This is a yield of 15 signatures per letter.

On 12 February 1958 the columnist Fulton Lewis, Jr., in his column published in many papers, asked: "Which organizations or individuals helped Dr. Pauling in his worldwide operation? Also, such a petition costs money; lots of it. Experts tell me that the expense would average

$10 per signature. It is certainly not amiss for a congressional committee to inquire who raised the necessary $100,000."

Who are Mr. Lewis's experts? They seem not to understand this issue—they greatly overestimated the cost of getting the signatures of scientists to an appeal urging an international agreement to stop bomb tests. It was about three cents per signature, instead of ten dollars.

However, I have been told by people with experience in gathering signatures by mail that a yield of one signature in ten letters is not unusual in such a campaign. The yield that I obtained, 15 signatures per letter, was accordingly 150 times the ordinary yield. I think that this result can be interpreted only as meaning that the scientists of the world are indeed greatly concerned about the problem of nuclear testing and nuclear war, and that this great concern is responsible for their enthusiastic cooperation.

The cost of gathering the 7500 signatures of scientists outside the United States amounted to about $250.00, which I expended for stationery, postage, and secretarial help. I am happy to be able to make this small contribution to the solution of world problems. I am, of course, pleased that the signatures were obtained at the bargain rate of about three cents per signature.

My wife and I have expended altogether about $600 on the appeal and petition, for gathering signatures, preparing material for press conferences and lists for distribution to the National Missions to the U.N., etc. This sum covered most of the cost of the whole job.

In December I was invited by the American Nobel Anniversary Committee to be present at their annual dinner, to be held in the Waldorf-Astoria Hotel in New York on the evening of 11 January 1958. I was asked also to take part in the program that evening, together with several other Nobel Laureates: Lord Boyd Orr of Great Britain, Mr. Lester Pearson of Canada, Miss Pearl Buck, and Dr. Albert Szent-Györgyi. Dr. Clarence Pickett, who as Executive Secretary of the American Friends Service Committee had received the Nobel Prize for Peace that was given to that organization, was also a participant in the program. I accepted the invitation.

I had been wondering what to do with the 9000 signatures of scientists, from all over the world, that had reached me by that time. It occurred to me that the thing to do with the appeal was to present it as a petition to the United Nations.

On arrival in New York I telephoned the United Nations, asked Mr. Hammarskjold's secretary for an appointment with Mr. Hammarskjold, and explained my purpose. I was given the appointment for noon on 13 January 1958, and at that time my wife and I visited Mr. Hammarskjold and presented the petition to him.

The Signers of the Petition

Among the signers of the petition are many of the leading scientists of the world.

A list of the 37 Nobel Laureates who signed the petition has already been given. The names of a few of them are repeated in the following listings.

The National Academy of Sciences of the United States of America is a distinguished organization, founded by an Act of Congress in 1864. It has, according to its charter, the obligation to advise the government of the United States about scientific matters, when requested by the government to do so.

The National Academy of Sciences has about 500 members. Of these a total of 104, one fifth, are among the signers. Their names and professions are listed in Appendix 4.

Ninety-five Fellows of the Royal Society of London, which lists among its members all of the leading scientists of the British Commonwealth, signed the petition. Among this group are Sir Henry Dale, a former president of the Royal Society and of the Royal Institution of Great Britain, and Sir Charles Darwin, former director of the National Physical Laboratory.

Among the signers of the petition were 216 leading scientists of the Soviet Union. This group includes Professor N. Semenov, Nobel Laureate in chemistry in 1956; also Professor A. Nesmeyanov, the distinguished chemist who is President of the Academy of Sciences of the U.S.S.R., Professor A. Topchiev, the chemist who is Secretary of the Academy of Sciences, Professor P. Kapitza, well known physicist who is a Foreign Associate of the National Academy of Sciences of the United States and a Fellow of the Royal Society of London, and many other scientists with world-wide reputations.

The numbers of the signers in each of the countries represented, as of May 1958, are given in the following list. There is an interesting variability in the response from the foreign countries, which probably is accidental in its origin—dependent upon the nature of the response of the usually three or four scientists in each country to whom my letters were addressed.

Number of Signers of the Petition, by Countries

Argentina	56	Japan	1,161
Australia	8	Jordan	11
Austria	1	Lebanon	1
Belgian Congo	6	Mexico	23
Belgium	43	Netherlands	29
Brazil	152	New Zealand	119
Bulgaria	392	Norway	112
Burma	50	Panama	2
Canada	24	Peru	1
Ceylon	27	Poland	86
China	4	Portugal	1
Colombia	34	Rumania	2,749
Czechoslovakia	284	South Africa	41
Denmark	53	Spain	7
Ecuador	13	Sweden	2
Egypt	236	Switzerland	13
France	463	Thailand	20
Germany	151	Turkey	5
Ghana	1	Uruguay	9
Great Britain	701	U.S.A.	2,875
Greece	1	U.S.S.R.	216
India	535	Venezuela	19
Ireland	9	West Pakistan	1
Israel	57	Yugoslavia	38
Italy	179	Total	11,021

9
The Need for International Agreements

I dread any national policy that depends upon ever greater power of destruction, ever greater arsenals of nuclear weapons. Such a policy, followed by two great nations, is sure to lead to catastrophe for the world.

The United States and the U.S.S.R. now have stockpiles of nuclear weapons that can destroy the world. Great Britain also has a stockpile.

So long as these weapons are in the hands of only three powers an agreement for their control is feasible. If testing continues and the possession of these weapons spreads to additional governments, the danger of outbreak of a cataclysmic nuclear war through the reckless action of some irresponsible national leader or through a technological or psychological accident will be greatly increased.

It may already be too late to prevent the spread of nuclear weapons to at least one more nation. France, which for some years has had an active nuclear-weapon program, may object to making such an agreement until some tests of her new weapons have been carried out.

Nevertheless, there is still a chance that such an agreement can be made. There is even the possibility that the nuclear weapons could be restricted to two great powers,

179

the United States and the U.S.S.R. There has been strong opposition in Great Britain to the possession of nuclear weapons by that commonwealth, and there is some possibility that Great Britain would voluntarily relinquish her store of the weapons.

The war between France and Algeria has been bitterly fought. If France were to obtain possession of nuclear weapons and the war with Algeria were to remain unsettled there is danger that she would be tempted to use them in this war. Such use might invoke nuclear retaliation from the U.S.S.R. and might be enough to start the Third World War.

There has also been discussion of providing nuclear arms to West Germany or of locating nuclear weapons in West Germany. The possibility cannot be ruled out of the existence, at some time in the near future, of a unified Germany. A prosperous German nation might, before many years have gone by, have its own stockpile of thousands of great nuclear weapons, enough to destroy the world—comparable in size to the American and Russian stockpiles. If the future world were to be a world of power politics, a world of world anarchy, as in the past, rather than of world government, there might arise in it a Germany armed with nuclear weapons and controlled by a successor to Hitler, a madman who would sacrifice the world to his nationalism.

With stockpiles of tens of thousands of nuclear weapons in the world, presumably some of them small ones, similar to the Hiroshima and Nagasaki bombs, there is the possibility that a considerable supply of the small weapons, so-called tactical weapons, would be stored ready for use in some nation, an ally of the United States or the U.S.S.R., where they could be captured by an unscrupulous national government. The job of manufacturing fissionable material for these bombs, uranium-235 or plutonium-239, is a moderately difficult one, which might not be undertaken lightly by a small nation. However, these small atomic bombs can easily be converted into superbombs. All that is needed is a supply of the fusionable materials lithium and deuterium and a supply of ordinary uranium, easily available in ton lots.

An additional danger is introduced by the possibility of development of power plants based on controlled fusion. Much research is now being carried out on this problem, and significant progress was reported a few months ago by groups of workers in Great Britain, the U.S., and other countries. This effort, if successful, would result in a great boon to the world, because the supply of fuel (deuterium) is inexhaustible, and, moreover, the operation of the power plants would not be attended by the serious problem of disposal of the immense quantities of radioactive materials and possibility of disastrous distribution of radioactive materials as a result of accident that attends the operation of fission power plants. But controlled-fusion power plants would introduce the danger that small nations could use the neutrons supplied by them to convert uranium into plutonium. The chemical process of purifying the plutonium is so simple that a small nation could undertake it, and in this way make its supply of fission bombs.

It might turn out in the course of time that scores of nations in the world would be able to develop good-sized stockpiles of weapons of 20-megaton size, capable of destroying the greatest cities in the world. There is the possibility of outbreak of nuclear banditry.

The nature of nuclear war is such that delay by even a

few hours in meeting an attack might make retaliation impossible. Decision about initiating the counterattack cannot be postponed until the time when the Commander-in-Chief can be informed; it must be invested in the various subordinate commanders. With increase in the number of people with power to launch the planes and missiles with their loads of superbombs, there comes greater and greater chance that a mistake will be made, that a nuclear war will be started because of an error.

Already, two planes loaded with H-bombs have crashed. In one case there was an explosion of the molecular explosive that serves to compress the fissionable material and initiate the nuclear explosion, but the nuclear explosion, fortunately, did not occur.

Even though great care is taken there is danger that, in the course of time, an accident will take place resulting in the detonation of a superbomb over a city or other target, and initiating the nuclear attack and counterattack that would bring disaster to the world.

An international agreement to stop the testing of nuclear weapons could serve as a first step toward a more general disarmament and the ultimate effective abolition of nuclear weapons, averting the possibility of a nuclear war that would be a catastrophe to all humanity.

The Present Situation

At the present time the East and the West do not differ very much about the conditions under which an international agreement to stop bomb tests could be made. Such an agreement is feasible in the near future.

The beginning of negotiations about international control of nuclear weapons came in June 1947, when the

Baruch plan for an international atomic energy commission was proposed to the Atomic Disarmament Commission by the United States. This plan was not acceptable to Russia, which was bargaining from a position of weakness. It was not until two years later that their first nuclear weapons were made in the U.S.S.R.

Little progress in the negotiations took place until after the death of Stalin in 1953. Since that time there has been a rough equality in military power between the East and the West. It is only during a period of such rough equality that effective negotiation between the great nations of the world can be initiated. The great deterrent to negotiation is fear—the fear that the enemy will capture control of the world through force.

It would be very dangerous for the world to be completely divided into two opposing camps. The existence of independent groups of nations, uncommitted to the U.S.S.R. or the United States, is important for world safety.

Since 1952 the Disarmament Commission of the United Nations, considering both nuclear weapons and conventional weapons, has discussed many alternative proposals about disarmament. As year has followed year the Russian proposals and the Western proposals have approached one another more and more closely.

The negotiations in the Disarmament Commission during recent years have been complex, with discussion not only of control and abolition of nuclear weapons but also of reduction in the conventional armed forces, cessation of nuclear tests, with systems of inspection, stopping of manufacture and conversion of nuclear stockpiles, systems of aerial inspections of various regions, and nuclear disarmament of a buffer zone in Europe, including West Germany, East Germany, Poland and other countries.

In June 1957 the United States proposed that disarmament take place in three stages. In the first stage the conventional forces should be reduced to two and one-half million each in Russia, China, and the United States, with further reduction to 2,100,000 in the second stage and to 1,700,000 in the third stage. The present levels of forces are probably about 4 million in the U.S.S.R., less than 3 million in the U.S., and somewhat more than 3 million in China.

The cessation of testing of nuclear weapons, with a system of inspection stations in each country manned by inspectors of other countries, would go into operation in the first stage. In July 1957 Russia accepted this proposal and agreed to a cessation of bomb tests, with a system of internal inspection stations. In the meantime the United States had included in its proposal the requirement that there be also a cessation of the manufacture of nuclear weapons, with a system of controls. As the negotiations continued through August 1957 there was disagreement about the areas which would be subjected to aerial inspection of the degree of conventional disarmament, and negotiations have remained essentially blocked since then.

At present the situation is that the U.S.S.R. has agreed to cessation of bomb tests, with a system of internal inspection stations, and some conventional disarmament in three stages, as described above. The position of the United States has been rather closely similar, except that the additional requirement has been made that the agreement should include the cessation of further stockpiling of nuclear weapons, with a system of controls.

I believe that the amount of agreement between these

proposals is so great that it should be possible through negotiation to resolve the differences between them.

In March 1958 the U.S.S.R., after completing a series of nuclear tests that included some great superbombs, announced that she was suspending nuclear tests indefinitely, but reserved the right to reconsider if any other nation carried out tests. The U.S. and Great Britain have also carried out tests in the spring of 1958.

Mr. Stassen and Mr. Dulles

For two years Mr. Harold E. Stassen, representing President Eisenhower, served as the chief United States negotiator in the U.N. disarmament discussions in London. He made great progress in clarifying the position of the United States on disarmament, and it seems likely that the breakdown of the negotiations is to be attributed not to him, but to the intervention of Mr. Dulles, the Secretary of State. The breakdown came in August 1957, when Mr. Dulles flew to London and participated in the discussion of the question of the areas of aerial inspection. His failure to reach a compromise with the U.S.S.R. representatives about the difference of opinion as to the regions to be covered by aerial inspection was an important factor in causing the conference to end.

Mr. Stassen resigned his post in February 1958. After Mr. Stassen's resignation the conduct of negotiations about disarmament was transferred from the President's office to the Department of State.

Some explanation of the attitude of the Secretary of State toward the execution of an international agreement to stop the testing of nuclear weapons, together with other aspects of disarmament, may be obtained from an address given in the University of Minnesota in March 1958 by Mr. Robert E. Matteson, who serves as Director of the White House Disarmament Staff. He discussed two policies, the first of which we may attribute to Mr. Stassen and the second to Secretary of State Dulles.

The first policy is described in the following words: "The first or 'relaxation of tension' is one which would recognize the strength of the Soviet bloc and would do more to encourage the liberalizing tendencies within the bloc. It would accept the Soviet as an equal power and would encourage the gradual evolution of the Soviet system toward freedom.

"The second or 'increased pressure,' on the other hand, is one which would emphasize the weakness of the Soviet bloc, would look toward pressuring the Soviet leaders into agreements which represent concessions by the Soviets, and would look toward striving to pressure the Soviet system into a collapse without a war."

It seems to me to be unrealistic to think that the West can apply such pressure to the U.S.S.R. as to lead to an overthrow of the government. In the same way, it seems to me to be unrealistic for Russian leaders to think that pressure applied to the United States will lead to the overthrow of the capitalistic system in this country, although it may be that Stalin had some such idea. I believe that the government in the U.S.S.R. has shown itself to be a stable government, but that the political system in the U.S.S.R. is slowly changing, and that we may hope that as the years go by there will be a steadily increasing acceptance in the U.S.S.R., as well as in other countries in the world, of the principles of democracy and human rights, a steady improvement in the social and political systems.

In the meantime the threat of nuclear catastrophe remains great. Nothing must be allowed to prevent the formulation and acceptance of a series of international agreements that would decrease the danger of nuclear catastrophe to the world.

At the time that this book is being written (March 1958) there are newspaper reports that the Eisenhower Administration is planning to review and perhaps to revise the United States policy about an international agreement with Russia to suspend nuclear weapons tests. It is reported that President Eisenhower and Secretary of State Dulles may drop their insistence that such an agreement include the cessation of production of nuclear explosives. It is this requirement that the U.S.S.R. objected to, possibly because of the great difficulty of devising an adequate system of controls. With this change in U.S. policy, the Russians probably would be willing to make an agreement.

Is Inspection Possible?

One objection that has been raised from time to time to the execution of an international agreement for cessation of all nuclear tests is that the U.S.S.R. would not abide by the agreement, and that they could carry out tests that would remain undetected.

I believe that it would be possible for scientists to devise a system of inspection stations such that no significant test of nuclear weapons could be carried out and remain undetected.

The detection of nuclear tests by monitoring the atmosphere for radioactivity is a well-known method. The U.S. AEC authorities seem to have no difficulty in detecting Russian tests; the Russian tests are regularly announced to the press by the AEC rather than by Russian authorities.

The Japanese scientists who monitor radioactivity not only discover that a test has been made, but describe the nature of the tested weapon, on the basis of their analysis of the fallout radioactivity. It surely would be possible to devise a system of stations that could carry out inspection and detect the radioactivity from even very small nuclear weapons.

The detonation of nuclear weapons underground has been suggested as a way to avoid detection. Such a weapon was detonated in Nevada on 19 September 1957. It was a weapon of the smallest size, 1.7 kilotons.

The first official account of this underground nuclear test was released on 6 March 1958 by the AEC. It contained the following statement: "When the device was detonated, only a few persons who witnessed the event from the forward control area, two and one-half miles from the ground zero, felt any earth shock, and off-site the earth movement was so slight that it could be recorded only on an extremely sensitive seismological instrument. The earth waves were recorded at seismological stations at Los Angeles, about 250 miles airlines from the shot mesa. This was the maximum distance at which the shot was recorded."

However, it was pointed out by I. F. Stone that *The New York Times* had reported on 20 September 1957 that the test had been detected by seismologists in Toronto and in Rome, and that U.S. Government seismologists also had detected the test in Fairbanks, Alaska, 2320 miles away, and in other seismological stations.

The news release by the AEC seems to have been written in such a way as to support the idea that an underground test might be carried out and remain undetected. The error by a factor of 10 in the distance at which the test was observed is interesting as an example of a mistake (described by the AEC as "inadvertent") made by this great organization.

The following statement by Professor Jay Orear of the Department of Physics of Columbia University (*Life* Magazine, 3 March 1958) is pertinent:

"As a member of the Columbia University Inspection Project who studied the technical problem of detecting nuclear tests, I strongly disagree with Dr. [Edward] Teller's claim that such tests can be effectively hidden if appropriate care is taken to hide them.

"One of the purposes of my study was to devise the minimal inspection scheme which could detect any violation of a test-ban agreement. The inspection system recommended in my report calls for about 25 U.N. monitoring stations, uniformly distributed through the U.S.S.R. This plus a provision that U.N. inspectors be invited to all large chemical explosions should make it possible to detect all nuclear tests unless they are of such ultra low yield as to be in the class of World War II blockbusters."

I myself think that no significant nuclear tests can be carried out without detection, in case that a proper system of inspection stations is set up by the United Nations.

Can We Trust the Russians?

One argument sometimes given against making international agreements is that we cannot trust the Russians.

We do not trust the Russians at the present time—we have great stockpiles of weapons, designed to be used against them. But we live in the same world with the Russians and, now that the world has become a nuclear world, we must learn to get along with them.

The proposed international agreement for stopping all

testing of nuclear weapons does not involve our trusting the Russians or the Russians' trusting us. In the discussions, both the U.S.S.R. and the U.S. have accepted the plan of having an effective system of inspection stations within the countries involved, manned by inspectors from other countries.

I am reminded of the time when I was with Lord Boyd Orr, former head of the Food and Agriculture Organization of the United Nations, and he was asked the question "Do you trust the Russian Foreign Office?"

His reply to this question was "I do not trust any foreign office, not even my own!"

The world of nations at the present time is largely anarchistic. Nations make agreements, treaties, with one another, and each nation keeps these agreements, its treaties, so long as they are of benefit to it—then it breaks them. In the past there has been no penalty.

The stage of development of the world now is such that it is becoming more and more important to every nation in the world that international agreements be made and be kept. There are many agreements that can be made that would benefit all of the nations in the world, for all time.

One of these agreements is the agreement to stop the testing of all nuclear weapons. Another is an agreement to stop further stockpiling of nuclear weapons, with an effective system of international controls. Another, of equal importance, is an agreement about development and control of missiles, especially intercontinental ballistic missiles. These missiles, by decreasing to a quarter of an hour the time elapsing between the pressing of the button that initiates the attack and the wreaking of destruction on the enemy, make essential, in the absence of international control, a finger-on-the-trigger attitude, with its great danger of accidental start of nuclear war.

In the course of time, as other agreements about disarmament are made, agreements such as to benefit all of the nations and all of the people of the world, there can be built up around these agreements a system of international law and mutual trust and confidence that will be a boon to mankind.

The development of such a system of international law has, of course, already been begun. The United Nations in its operation is an illustration of it.

With every year of successful operation of the United Nations the system of international law becomes more effective. As more nations are added to the group within the United Nations—especially when China becomes a member nation—the United Nations will become more powerful, and the system of international law will become more and more effective.

As more and more agreements about disarmament and other international problems are made, we must at first continue to mistrust Russia—and Russia must continue to mistrust us. Each step toward the world of the future must be taken carefully—yet *it must be taken.*

The situation has been summarized by Dr. Harrison Brown, Professor of Geochemistry in the California Institute of Technology, in a lecture that he gave in March, as follows:

"I am convinced that if the Soviet Union were, by some magic, to disappear tomorrow, our situation would not be greatly eased. I am convinced that, as industrialization continues its relentless spread within the framework of international anarchy, we are going to be faced by new Germanies, new Japans, and new Soviet Unions.

"Of all of our short-range goals, the one of overwhelming urgency, it seems to me, is to secure agreements which would make it extremely difficult for the Soviet Union and the United States to engage in large-scale nuclear war and which would severely hinder, if not completely stop, the spread of nuclear technology to the rest of the world. Dr. Teller believes that any such agreements would be to our disadvantage because we could not be certain that the Soviet Union might not 'bootleg' tests. I challenge this view, and in doing so I do not stand alone in the scientific world."

I myself believe that it is possible for us to secure agreements with the Soviet Union to stop tests and to achieve disarmament and I believe further that the agreements could be of such a nature that the Soviet Union would adhere to them because it would be very much to her advantage to do so.

Morality

The scientists' petition to the United Nations says "We have in common with our fellow men a deep concern for the welfare of all human beings."

The petition is a plea that the tests of nuclear weapons be stopped immediately by effective international agreement, both to prevent further damage to the health of human beings and to the human race and as a first step toward averting nuclear war.

Sometimes I think that I am dreaming; I can hardly believe that the world is as it is. The world is beautiful, wonderful—scientists every year uncover, discover, more and more wonders of organic and inorganic nature. Man is a wonderful organism—the human body, with its millions of millions of cells, molecules of many different kinds entering into chemical reactions with one another; the human mind, capable of feats of complex calculation, of abstract reasoning infinitely beyond those of even the greatest giant electronic calculator.

Man has developed admirable principles of morality, which in large part govern the actions of individual human beings. And yet, we are murderers, mass murderers. Almost all of us, even many of our religious leaders, accept with equanimity a world policy of devoting a large part of our world income, our world resources—one hundred billion dollars a year—to the cold-blooded readying of nuclear weapons to kill hundreds of millions of people, to damage the pool of human germ plasm in such a way that after a great nuclear war our descendants might be hardly recognizable as human beings.

Does the Commandment "Thou Shalt Not Kill" mean nothing to us? Are we to interpret it as meaning "Thou shalt not kill except on the grand scale," or "Thou shalt not kill except when the national leaders say to do so"?

I am an American, deeply interested in the welfare of my fellow Americans, of our great Nation. But I am first of all a human being. I believe in *morality*. Even if it were possible (which it is not) to purchase security for the United States of America by killing all of the hundreds of millions of people behind the Iron Curtain without doing any harm to anyone else, I would not be willing that it be done.

I believe that there is a greater power in the world than the evil power of military force, of nuclear bombs—there is the power of *good,* of *morality,* of *humanitarianism.*

I believe in the power of the human spirit. I should like to see our great Nation, the United States of America, take the lead in the fight for good, for peace, against the evil of war. I should like to see in our cabinet a Secretary for Peace, with a budget of billions of dollars per year, perhaps as much as 10 percent of the amount now expended for military purposes. I should like to see set up a great international research program involving thousands of scientists, economists, geographers, and other experts working steadily year after year in the search for possible solutions to world problems, ways to prevent war and to preserve peace.

During the past hundred years there have been astounding developments in science and technology, developments that have completely changed the nature of the world in which we live. So far as I can see, the nature of diplomacy, of the conduct of international affairs, has changed very little.

The time has now come for this aspect of the world to change, because we now recognize that the power to destroy the world is a power that cannot be used.

May our great Nation, the United States of America, be the leader in bringing *morality* into its proper place of prime importance in the conduct of world affairs!

10
A Proposal:
Research for Peace

How is peace in the world to be achieved? How are the great world problems to be solved, without resort to war, war that would now lead to catastrophe, to world suicide?

I propose that the great world problems be solved in the way that other problems are solved—by working hard to find their solution—by carrying on *research for peace*.

Research consists in striving in every possible way to discover what the facts are, to learn more and more about the nature of the world, and to use all information that can be obtained in the effort to find the solution to difficult problems.

As the world has become more and more complex in recent centuries and decades there has developed a greater and greater reliance upon specialists to carry on research and to make discoveries.

Much research in science and in other fields of knowledge is carried out by professors in the universities of the world, together with their students and associates. Much of the research done in the universities is fundamental research, not designed to lead directly to the solution of a particular practical problem. It has often turned out, however, that discoveries made in the course of fundamental research have had an immediate practical application. Still more often, these discoveries have formed the foundation for later discoveries that were put to use in the solution of important practical problems.

An example of the way in which the world has progressed through research is provided by the discovery of penicillin.

Dr. Alexander Fleming, Professor of Bacteriology in the University of London, was carrying on some studies of the growth of bacteria in his laboratory. A spot of mold began to grow on the surface of the agar plate in one of the dishes in which he was growing a bacterial culture. He noticed that the bacteria did not grow in the region immediately around the spot of mold, and he was curious to find out why. He discovered that the mold manufactured a substance with the power of stopping the growth of the bacteria. Later Dr. Howard Florey and Dr. Ernst B. Chain of Oxford University purified the substance, penicillin, and demonstrated its great effectiveness in the control of infectious diseases.

This discovery has revolutionized medical practice and has been of the greatest value to the human race in decreasing the amount of human suffering.

Another example is provided by the many basic discoveries that led to the development of methods of controlled release of nuclear energy and that brought the world into the nuclear age.

These discoveries were difficult to make because they could not be predicted. Nobody planned that Roentgen should discover x-radiation, that Becquerel should discover radioactivity, that Madame Marie Curie and Professor Pierre Curie should discover radium, that Einstein should discover the theory of relativity, which, by giving the relation between mass and energy, provided the theoretical basis for the later work on nuclear energy.

Nobody planned that James Chadwick should discover the neutron, that Irene Joliot-Curie and her husband Frederic Joliot should discover how to make artificial radioactive elements, that Enrico Fermi should discover how to produce nuclear reactions with very heavy elements by irradiating them with neutrons, that Otto Hahn, Felix Strassmann, and Lise Meitner should discover that some of these reactions involved the fission of heavy nuclei.

No director of research, no board of directors can plan such a program of fundamental research. Some of the most important discoveries have been so strange, so unexpected, that they have burst upon a surprised world without anticipation. They have required the genius, the flight of imagination, the boldness of thought of a single investigator for their conception.

Most of these great discoveries have been made by scientists who have devoted their lives to carrying on research, to the effort to discover something new about the world. And often the attack on a single problem has been stubbornly carried out year after year by a scientist, for many years.

At the present time hundreds of theoretical physicists all over the world are attacking the problem of the structure of the nuclei of atoms. No one knows just how the 235 nucleons, 92 protons and 243 neutrons, that are grouped together within the nucleus of uranium-235 are arranged, what sort of motions they carry out, how they interact with one another. There is no satisfactory theory of the structure of nuclei.

The theoretical physicists have been working hard on

this problem for 25 years, and at the same time thousands of experimental physicists have been gathering facts about nuclear structure.

All of these scientists hope that some one will solve the problem. They are sure that it will be solved, but they do not know whether it will be necessary to work five years more, or ten years more, or 25 years more to find the solution. It is a difficult problem; but the scientists know that it will be solved, in the course of time.

Applied Research

In addition to the thousands of university professors and other research men who are carrying on fundamental research, there are tens of thousands of scientists who are working in industrial laboratories and government laboratories, a few also in university laboratories, on applied research, the application of discoveries that have been made in the effort to solve important practical problems. It has been estimated that applied research is being carried out in the United States at a rate corresponding to an expenditure of about 4 billion dollars per year. It accordingly constitutes about 1 percent of our national effort. Both fundamental research and applied research are being carried out in the U.S.S.R. and other nations on a roughly corresponding scale.

Many features of the modern world are the result of applied research. Telephones, electric lights, radio, television, synthetic fibers and textiles, new alloys, jet planes, machines of many kinds have been developed in this way.

The design of nuclear power plants is an example of applied research. Another example is the design of atomic bombs, hydrogen bombs, and superbombs.

Some of the important practical problems are so difficult that the attack on them must be carried out for years. Some of the great industrial corporations support research laboratories in which long-term projects are attacked, together with simpler projects involving the solution of practical problems. Some fundamental scientific discoveries have been made in these industrial laboratories.

Medical research provides another example of applied research of great importance to the world. The National Cancer Institute, the National Heart Institute, and other branches of the National Institutes of Health of the U.S. Public Health Service employ thousands of scientists who, in various ways, are attacking the diseases that cause a large amount of human suffering.

The attack on the cancer problem has been going on for decades, and will continue to go on. The problem is a very difficult one, but scientists are confident that, in the course of time, great progress can be made in its solution.

The world progresses through research.

Research for War

During recent decades greater and greater use has been made of research and of the services of scientists and other scholars in the conduct of war and the preparation for war.

The Second World War was fought almost entirely with weapons and by methods developed by scientists.

Armaments of the great nations of the world are now much different from those upon which they relied during the Second World War. The changes—the development of nuclear weapons, of jet planes, of guided missiles, of ballistic missiles, of improved radar and other methods of detection—have resulted from scientific research, both fundamental and applied.

Even the tactical and strategic techniques are now developed through research. During the Second World War the admirals and generals came to rely more and more upon advice from scientists and other specialists constituting their operations analysis groups. These groups of mathematicians, physicists, chemists, and other specialists are able to develop a far deeper understanding of modern warfare than the admirals and generals, to analyze the problems involved, and to give advice as to how war should be conducted that is far better than the conclusions that the admirals and generals themselves could reach.

These specialists devote years to the attack on the problem of how best to wage war. They make use of giant electronic computers to assist them in their attack. It may well be that some of these able men have found some imaginative and unexpected solutions to some of the military problems.

Great sums of money, hundreds of millions of dollars per year, are now being spent on research for war, and many thousands of scientists and other specialists are involved in this work.

An example of a research organization of this sort is the Rand Corporation, in Santa Monica, California. This corporation employs many scientists and other specialists who work on the problems of defense, of preparing for war, and of waging war.

Also, special projects relating to research on methods of defense and methods of waging war are set up under the auspices of universities and technical schools. These projects may cost many millions of dollars, and many able scientists in the world may be attracted into taking part in them.

Research for Peace

The time has now come for the greatest of all problems facing the world, the problem of peace, to be attacked in an effective way.

I propose that there be set up a great research organization, the World Peace Research Organization, within the structure of the United Nations.

The duty of the World Peace Research Organization would be to attack the problem of preserving the peace, to carry out research on preserving peace in the world, to carry out research on peace. This would mean, of course, carrying out research on how to solve great world problems, problems of the kind that have in the past led to war. It would also involve attacking the problem of how to prevent the outbreak of a nuclear war by design or by accident.

The World Peace Research Organization, if it existed today, could make a thorough analysis of the problems involved in an international agreement to stop all testing of nuclear weapons. It could, after making its study, propose a system that, in the opinion of the Organization, would have the greatest safety, the smallest chance of violation by any nation, would be of the maximum benefit to all of the nations and all of the people of the world. Such a proposal would without doubt be given serious consideration by the nations of the world.

The World Peace Research Organization should be a large one. It should include many scientists, representing all fields of science, and many other specialists—economists, geographers, specialists in all fields of knowledge.

In order that these important problems might be attacked with the aid of the advice and help of some of the most able men in the world, satisfactory conditions for work would have to be provided for these men. This means that the facilities and environment would have to be similar to those in the great universities, and the outstanding authorities in various fields would have to be allowed to prosecute their studies in a fundamental and thorough way. They would, however, be at hand to help with special projects, attacks on special problems, when needed.

The multiplicity of the fields of human knowledge pertinent to the problem of peace and the complexity of the problem itself are such that the Organization should have thousands of specialists on its staff. Within two years after its inception the Organization might have a staff of about 2000 specialists, and within 10 years its staff might have increased to 10,000 specialists, plus the other staff members necessary for it to function effectively.

The specialists on the staff of the Organization should have freedom to attack the problem of peace in the world comparable to that with which professors in a university are free to attack the problems in which they are interested. They should be provided with assistants, laboratories, and other facilities of such a nature as to permit them to work most effectively.

There would be large numbers of postdoctoral research men attracted to the Organization, to work in association with its senior members, and satisfactory facilities for them would have to be provided.

I think, however, that no arrangement would be made for students working for a degree, not even for the doctor's degree. In this respect the Organization would differ from a university; it would instead resemble the Institute for

Advanced Study in Princeton, New Jersey, but would be much larger.

The appointment of specialists to the World Peace Research Organization of the United Nations should be on essentially the same basis as appointment to professorial positions in the leading universities. The senior men should be given appointments with tenure comparable to academic tenure in universities and to civil service in government service.

We cannot expect that the great problems in the modern world can be solved in an easy way by government officials who have many duties and who cannot devote to the problems the long and careful thought that they require for their solution. These problems need to be attacked in the way that other problems are attacked in the modern world—by research, carried out by people who think about the problems year after year.

There are great possibilities of progress in this way. If thousands of outstandingly able investigators are attacking the world problems by imaginative and original methods, working on these problems year after year, many of these problems should be solved.

It is possible that some great discoveries may be made, discoveries that would so change the world as to make the danger of outbreak of a nuclear war far less than it is at present.

The cost of supporting the World Peace Research Organization within the United Nations on the scale described, with at first 2000 specialists and many auxiliary members of the staff, increasing to 10,000 specialists in ten years, would be of the order of magnitude of 25 million dollars per year at the beginning and 100 million dollars per year ultimately.

203

This cost is very small in comparison with the sums expended for military purposes. The military budget of the United States at the present time is about $40,000,000,000 and that of Russia and other countries is comparable, so that we may estimate the total cost to the world of the military machines at the present time as about 100,000 million dollars per year. The cost of the proposed World Peace Research Organization within the United Nations would be only about one-tenth of one percent of this sum.

The damage that would be done to the world by a nuclear war is inestimable. What, in dollars, would be the loss to the United States if half of our people were killed? What, in dollars, would be the property damage to the United States if New York, Chicago, Philadelphia, Los Angeles, and scores of other cities were destroyed? We might say that the property damage would amount to several million million dollars. If there were a chance of one in one hundred thousand of preventing this damage, it would be well worth while to do so. It would be well worth while to pay the corresponding sum, 100 million dollars, to prevent the loss. The World Peace Research Organization would be a cheap insurance policy.

There is no doubt in my mind that the World Peace Research Organization would be able to make suggestions about international problems that would be accepted by the nations of the world and that would lead to a significant decrease in the armaments budget. The military budget of the United States might well be decreased, as a result of these suggestions, from 40 billion dollars to 36 billion dollars per year, and then to 32 billion dollars per year, and then to 28 billion dollars per year, and so on, with an accompanying increase in national safety, rather than a decrease.

I have no doubt that the World Peace Research Organization would pay for itself in a short while.

The cost of preserving peace in the world would not, of course, be limited to the 100 million dollars per year for support of the World Peace Research Organization. Many of the international agreements that will be made in the future in connection with the solution of world problems by peaceful means will involve the expenditure of considerable sums of money. These sums for the United States might be of the order of magnitude of the four billion dollars per year now expended on foreign aid (including military as well as non-military aid). It may well be that, as the military budget is decreased by several billion dollars a year below its present figure of 40 billion dollars a year in the United States, a significant fraction of the decrease would be allocated to uses connected with the peaceful solution of world problems.

We may, however, anticipate that the world would benefit from these expenditures, and that the United States would benefit. We may expect that the standards of living in the world as a whole and in the United States in particular could be raised significantly. The military budgets of the countries of the world do not contribute to raising the standards of living. They represent almost entirely a waste of world resources, an expenditure of money without any corresponding return in the form of useful goods. A change in policy that leads to a reduction of the military budgets, with increased safety for the nations of the world, can only result in benefit to the people.

President Eisenhower in his address on 17 April 1957 pointed out that great things might be done with the sums of money now being spent on armaments. He mentioned that if the U.S. had spent only $50,000,000,000 on defense during the five years 1953 to 1958 rather than the $200,000,000,000 that was spent, we could have constructed the entire nationwide interstate system of highways that has been planned, built every worthwhile hydroelectric power project in America, built all the hospitals needed for the next ten years and all the schools needed for the next ten years, and have been able also to reduce the national debt by $50,000,000,000.

The World Peace Research Organization should be a research organization, which makes analyses of world problems, makes discoveries, and makes proposals. It should not be a policy-making organization.

One of the greatest of the problems facing the world, closely connected with the problem of war or peace, is the population problem. In eight years the United States has increased in population by over 12 percent, from 151 million in 1950 to an estimated 175 million in 1958. The population of the whole world is increasing at nearly the same rate. Much of the increase has been due to medical progress, in decreasing the infant and childhood mortality and lengthening the life span.

As the population pressure becomes greater in some countries in the world, the danger of the outbreak of war becomes greater. The population problem is one that should be attacked by the World Peace Research Organization.

Every great nation should also have its own peace research organization. Careful analyses would have to be made by the nations of the proposals made by the World Peace Research Organization. These analyses could be made only by similar groups of specialists. In the United States, for example, a Peace Research Organization might be set up under the Science Advisor to the President.

Another possibility is that it be incorporated within the Department of Peace, in case that a Secretary for Peace is added to the Cabinet. In either case, the Peace Research Organization of the United States should not be an operating organization or a policy-making organization, but a research organization.

At the present time Dr. James R. Killian is serving as Science Advisor to the President. He has appointed a staff of scientists as his advisors. They, however, are consultants, not full-time workers. Such an organization, the Science Advisor to the President and his group of part-time scientific consultants, represents a puny effort indeed for an attack on the great world problems, in which science plays such an important part.

It is not surprising that under these circumstances the President and other members of our government, as well as of other governments of the world, have a seriously incomplete understanding of the great world problems and are lacking in imagination in their attack on them.

The World Peace Research Organization should have its own buildings, located not in a city but in some rural or semi-rural community, suitable to its activities of slow, thoughtful attack on great problems, suitable to the search for the truth.

I believe that there would be no difficulty in obtaining the services in the World Peace Research Organization of many of the most able scientists and scholars in the world.

There is no doubt that many of the specialists who would be most effective in this work would also have the strongest emotional attraction to it. An added attraction would be that of association with the many other outstanding scientists and scholars of the world who would constitute its staff. In its intellectual environment the

Organization should be comparable to the greatest universities in the world.

The World of the Future

We live now in a period of rapid change—a period of revolution, of nuclear revolution. Everything in the world has been changed as a result of scientific discoveries. I think that the greatest change of all is that in the ways of waging war—the change from old-fashioned molecular explosives, the one-ton TNT bomb, to the great nuclear weapon, the superbomb that is twenty million times as powerful.

This change, from molecular explosives to superbombs, has caused war to rule itself out.

Even the politicians and diplomats are changing, although they are slow to show it. They still behave at times as though war were the method to solve international disputes, but it is clear that the leaders of the great nations know that a nuclear war cannot be allowed to wreak its destruction on the world.

The time has now come for war to be abandoned, for diplomacy to move out of the nineteenth century into the real world of the twentieth century, a world in which war and the threat of war no longer have a rightful place as the instrument of national policy. We must move towards a world governed by justice, by international law, and not by force.

We must all, including the diplomats and national leaders, change our point of view. We must recognize that extreme nationalism is a thing of the past. The idea that it is just as important to do harm to other nations as to do good for your own nation must be given up. We must all begin to work for the world as a whole, for humanity.

Science is the search for the truth—it is not a game in which one tries to beat his opponent, to do harm to others. We need to have the spirit of science in international affairs, to make the conduct of international affairs the effort to find the right solution, the just solution of international problems, not the effort by each nation to get the better of other nations, to do harm to them when it is possible.

I believe in morality, in justice, in humanitarianism. We must recognize now that the power to destroy the world by the use of nuclear weapons is a power that cannot be used—we cannot accept the idea of such monstrous immorality.

The time has now come for morality to take its proper place in the conduct of world affairs; the time has now come for the nations of the world to submit to the just regulation of their conduct by international law.

Appendixes

Appendix 1

"ONLY THEN SHALL WE FIND COURAGE"

BY ALBERT EINSTEIN

In an Interview with Michael Amrine

(Reprinted with permission from *The New York Times Magazine,* 23 June 1946)

Many persons have inquired concerning a recent message of mine that "a new type of thinking is essential if mankind is to survive and move to higher levels."

Often in evolutionary processes a species must adapt to new conditions in order to survive. Today the atomic bomb has altered profoundly the nature of the world as we know it, and the human race consequently finds itself in a new habitat to which it must adapt its thinking.

In the light of new knowledge, a world authority and an eventual world state are not just *desirable* in the name of brotherhood, they are *necessary* for survival. In previous ages a nation's life and culture could be protected to some extent by the growth of armies in national competition. Today we must abandon competition and secure cooperation. This must be the central fact in all our considerations of international affairs; otherwise we face certain disaster. Past thinking and methods did not prevent world wars. Future thinking *must* prevent wars.

Modern war, the bomb, and other discoveries present us with revolutionary circumstances. Never before was it possible for one nation to make war on another without sending armies across borders. Now with rockets and atomic bombs no center of population on the earth's surface is secure from surprise destruction in a single attack.

America has a temporary superiority in armament, but it is certain that we have no lasting secret. What nature tells one group of men, she will tell in time to any group interested and patient enough in asking the questions. But our temporary superiority gives this nation the tremendous responsibility of leading mankind's effort to surmount the crisis.

Being an ingenious people, Americans find it hard to believe there is no foreseeable defense against atomic bombs. But this is a basic fact. Scientists do not even know of any field which promises us any hope of adequate defense. The military-minded cling to old methods of thinking and one Army department has been surveying possibilities of going underground, and in wartime placing factories in places like Mammoth Cave. Others speak of dispersing our population centers into "linear" or "ribbon" cities.

Reasonable men with these new facts to consider refuse to contemplate a future in which our culture would attempt to survive in ribbons or in underground tombs. Neither is there reassurance in proposals to keep a hundred thousand men alert along the coasts scanning the sky with radar. There is no radar defense against the V-2, and should a "defense" be developed after years of research, it is not humanly possible for any defense to be perfect. Should one rocket with atomic warhead strike Minneapolis, that city would look almost exactly like Nagasaki.

Rifle bullets kill men, but atomic bombs kill cities. A tank is a defense against a bullet but there is no defense in science against the weapon which can destroy civilization.

Our defense is not in armaments, nor in science, nor in going underground. Our defense is in law and order.

Henceforth, every nation's foreign policy must be judged at every point by one consideration: does it lead us to a world of law and order or does it lead us back toward anarchy and death? I do not believe that we can prepare for war and at the same time prepare for a world community. When humanity holds in its hand the weapon with which it can commit suicide, I believe that to put more power into the gun is to increase the probability of disaster.

Remembering that our main consideration is to avoid this disaster, let us briefly consider international relations in the world today, and start with America. The war which began with Germany using weapons of unprecedented frightfulness against women and children ended with the United States using a supreme weapon killing thousands at one blow.

Many persons in other countries now look on America with great suspicion, not only for the bomb but because they fear she will become imperialistic. Before the recent turn in our policy I was sometimes not quite free from such fears myself.

Others might not fear Americans if they knew us as we know one another, honest and sober and neighbors. But in other countries they know that a sober nation can become drunk with victory. If Germany had not won a victory in 1870, what tragedy for the human race might have been averted!

We are still making bombs and the bombs are making

hate and suspicion. We are keeping secrets and secrets breed distrust. I do not say we should now turn the secret of the bomb loose in the world, but are we ardently seeking a world in which there will be no need for bombs or secrets, a world in which science and men will be free?

While we distrust Russia's secrecy and she distrusts ours we walk together to certain doom.

The basic principles of the Acheson-Lilienthal Report are scientifically sound and technically ingenious, but as Mr. Baruch wisely said, it is a problem not of physics but of ethics. There has been too much emphasis on legalisms and procedure; it is easier to denature plutonium than it is to denature the evil spirit of man.

The United Nations is the only instrument we have to work with in our struggle to achieve something better. But we have used U.N. and U.N. form and procedure to outvote the Russians on some occasions when the Russians were right. Yes, I do not think it is possible for any nation to be right all the time or wrong all the time. In all negotiations, whether over Spain, Argentina, Palestine, food or atomic energy, so long as we rely on procedure and keep the threat of military power, we are attempting to use old methods in a world which is changed forever.

No one gainsays that the United Nations Organization at times gives great evidence of eventually justifying the desperate hope that millions have in it. But time is not given to us in solving the problems science and war have brought. Powerful forces in the political world are moving swiftly toward crisis. When we look back to the end of the war—it seems ten years ago! Many leaders express well the need for world authority and an eventual world government, but actual planning and action to this end have been appallingly slow.

Private organizations anticipate the future, but government agencies seem to live in the past. In working away from nationalism toward a supra-nationalism, for example, it is obvious that the national spirit will survive longer in armies than anywhere else. This might be tempered in the United Nations military forces by mixing the various units together, but certainly not by keeping a Russian unit intact side by side with an intact American unit, with the usual inter-unit competition added to the national spirit of the soldiers in this world enforcement army. But if the military staffs of the U.N. are working out concrete proposals along these lines, for a true internationally minded force, I have yet to read of it.

Similarly, we are plagued in the present world councils over the question of representation. It does not seem fair to some, for example, that each small Latin-American nation should have a vote while much larger nations are also limited to one vote. On the other hand, representation on a population basis may seem unfair to the highly developed states, because surely great masses of ignorant, backward peoples should not carry as much voice in the complicated technology of our world as those with greater experience.

Fremont Rider in an excellent book, *The Great Dilemma of World Organizations,* discusses the idea of representation on the basis of education and literacy—number of teachers, physicians, and so on. Backward nations looking forward to greater power in the councils of men would be told, "To get more votes you must *earn* them."

These and a hundred other questions concerning the desirable evolution of the world seem to be getting very little attention. Meanwhile, men high in government propose defense or war measures which would not only compel us to live in a universal atmosphere of fear but would

217

cost untold billions of dollars and ultimately destroy our American free way of life—even before a war.

To retain even a temporary total security in an age of total war, government will have to secure total control. Restrictive measures will be required by the necessities of the situation, not through the conspiracy of wilful men. Starting with the fantastic guardianship now imposed on innocent physics professors, outmoded thinkers will insidiously change men's lives more completely than did Hitler, for the forces behind them will be more compelling.

Before the raid on Hiroshima, leading physicists urged the War Department not to use the bomb against defenseless women and children. The war could have been won without it. The decision was made in consideration of possible future loss of American lives—and now we have to consider possible loss in future atomic bombings of *millions of lives*. The American decision may have been a fatal error, for men accustom themselves to thinking that a weapon which was used once can be used again.

Had we shown other nations the test explosion at Alamogordo, New Mexico, we could have used it as an education for new ideas. It would have been an impressive and favorable moment to make considered proposals for world order to end war. Our renunciation of this weapon as too terrible to use would have carried great weight in negotiations and made convincing our sincerity in asking other nations for a binding partnership to develop these newly unleashed powers for good.

The old type of thinking can raise a thousand objections of "realism" against this simplicity. But such thought ignores the *psychological realities*. All men fear atomic war. All men hope for benefits from these new powers. Between the realities of man's true desires and the realities of man's

218

danger, what are the obsolete "realities" of protocol and military protection?

During the war many persons fell out of the habit of doing their own thinking, for many had to do simply what they were told to do. Today lack of interest would be a great error, for there is much the average man can do about this danger.

This nation held a great debate concerning the menace of the Axis, and again today we need a great chain reaction of awareness and communication. Current proposals should be discussed in the light of the basic facts, in every newspaper, in schools, churches, in town meetings, in private conversations, and neighbor to neighbor. Merely reading about the bomb promotes knowledge in the mind, but only talk between men promotes feelings in the heart.

Not even scientists completely understand atomic energy, for each man's knowledge is incomplete. Few men have ever seen the bomb. But all men if told a few facts can understand that this bomb and the danger of war is a very real thing, and not something far away. It directly concerns every person in the civilized world. We cannot leave it to generals, Senators, and diplomats to work out a solution over a period of generations. Perhaps five years from now several nations will have made bombs and it will be too late to avoid disaster.

Ignoring the realities of faith, good-will and honesty in seeking a solution, we place too much faith in legalisms, treaties, and mechanisms. We must begin through the U.N. Atomic Energy Commission to work for binding agreement, but America's decision will not be made over a table in the United Nations. Our representatives in New York, in Paris, or in Moscow depend ultimately on decisions made in the village square.

To the village square we must carry the facts of atomic energy. From there must come America's voice.

This belief of physicists prompted our formation of the Emergency Committee of Atomic Scientists, with headquarters at Princeton, N. J., to make possible a great national campaign for education on these issues. Detailed planning for world security will be easier when negotiators are assured of public understanding of our dilemmas.

Then our American proposals will be not merely documents about machinery, the dull, dry statements of a government to other governments, but the embodiment of a message to humanity from a nation of human beings.

Science has brought forth this danger, but the real problem is in the minds and hearts of men. We will not change the hearts of other men by mechanism, but by changing *our* hearts and speaking bravely.

We must be generous in giving to the world the knowledge we have of the forces of nature, after establishing safeguards against abuse.

We must be not merely willing but actively eager to submit ourselves to binding authority necessary for world security.

We must realize that we cannot simultaneously plan for war and peace.

When we are clear in heart and mind—only then shall we find courage to surmount the fear which haunts the world.

(The above statement by Professor Einstein was given wide circulation in 1946 in a pamphlet of the Emergency Committee of Atomic Scientists. The members of the Emergency Committee at that time were Albert Einstein (Chairman), Harold C. Urey (Vice-Chairman), Hans A.

Bethe, Selig Hecht, Thorfin R. Hogness, Philip Morse, Linus Pauling, Leo Szilard, and Victor F. Weisskopf. A few other scientists were later added to the group. It ceased to function in 1950, in part because of the strain it imposed on Professor Einstein.)

THE MAINAU DECLARATION
OF NOBEL LAUREATES

(Mainau, Lake of Constance, 15 July 1955)

We, the undersigned, are scientists of different countries, different creeds, different political persuasions. Outwardly, we are bound together only by the Nobel Prize, which we have been favored to receive. With pleasure we have devoted our lives to the service of science. It is, we believe, a path to a happier life for people. We see with horror that this very science is giving mankind the means to destroy itself. By total military use of weapons feasible today, the earth can be contaminated with radioactivity to such an extent that whole peoples can be annihilated. Neutrals may die thus as well as belligerents.

If war broke out among the great powers, who could guarantee that it would not develop into a deadly conflict? A nation that engages in a total war thus signals its own destruction and imperils the whole world.

We do not deny that perhaps today peace is being preserved precisely by the fear of these weapons. Nevertheless, we think it is a delusion if governments believe that they can avoid war for a long time through the fear of these weapons. Fear and tension have often engendered wars. Similarly it seems to us a delusion to believe that small conflicts could in the future always be decided by traditional weapons. In extreme danger no nation will deny

222

itself the use of any weapon that scientific technology can produce.

All nations must come to the decision to renounce force as a final resort of policy. If they are not prepared to do this they will cease to exist.

Lord Edgar Douglas Adrian, Cambridge
Kurt Alder, Köln
Max Born, Bad Pyrmont
Walther Bothe, Heidelberg
Percy William Bridgman, Cambridge
Adolf Butenandt, Tübingen
Arthur H. Compton, Saint Louis
Henrik Dam, Copenhagen
Clinton Joseph Davisson, Charlottesville
P. A. M. Dirac, Oxford
Edward A. Doisy, Saint Louis
Gerhard Domagk, Wuppertal
Joseph Erlanger, Saint Louis
Hans K. von Euler-Chelpin, Stockholm
James Franck, Chicago
Otto Hahn, Göttingen
Werner Heisenberg, Göttingen
P. S. Hench, Rochester, Minn.

Gustav Hertz, Leipzig
Georg von Hevesy, Stockholm
C. Heymans, Gent
Frédéric Joliot-Curie, Paris
Irène Joliot-Curie, Paris
E. C. Kendall, Princeton
Sir Hans Krebs, Oxford
Richard Kuhn, Heidelberg
Max von Laue, Berlin
Fritz Lipman, Boston
A. E. Moniz, Lisbon
Paul Hermann Müller, Basel
H. J. Muller, Bloomington
William Murphy, Boston
Wolfgang Pauli, Zurich
Linus Pauling, Pasadena
C. F. Powell, Bristol
Sir Chandrasekhara Venkata Raman, Bangalore
Th. Reichstein, Basel
Lord Bertrand Russell, Richmond
L. Ruzicka, Zurich
F. F. Sillanpää, Helsinki
Frederick Soddy, Brighton
W. M. Stanley, Berkeley

Hermann Staudinger, Freiburg

Richard Laurence Millington Synge, Bucksburn

Max Theiler, New York

A. Tiselius, Uppsala

Harold C. Urey, Chicago

G. H. Whipple, Rochester

Heinrich Wieland, Starnberg

Adolf Windaus, Göttingen

Hideki Yukawa, Kyoto

Frits Zernike, Groningen

Appendix 3

A DECLARATION OF CONSCIENCE

BY ALBERT SCHWEITZER

(Issued on 24 April 1957
under the auspices of the
Nobel Peace Prize Committee in Oslo.
Reprinted with permission from the author and
The Saturday Review, 18 May 1957)

Since March 1, 1954 hydrogen bombs have been tested
by the United States at the Pacific island of Bikini in the
Marshall group and by Soviet Russia in Siberia. We know
that testing of atomic weapons is something quite different
from testing of non-atomic ones. Earlier, when a new type
of giant gun had been tested, the matter ended with the
detonation. After the explosion of a hydrogen bomb that
is not the case. Something remains in the air, namely, an
incalculable number of radioactive particles emitting radioactive rays. This was also the case with the uranium bombs
dropped on Nagasaki and Hiroshima and those which were
subsequently tested. However, because these bombs were
of smaller size and less effectiveness compared with the
hydrogen bombs, not much attention was given to this fact.

Since radioactive rays of sufficient amount and strength
have harmful effects on the human body, it must be considered whether the radiation resulting from the hydrogen
explosions that have already taken place represents a dan-

ger which would increase with new explosions.

In the course of the three-and-a-half years that have passed since then [the test explosions of the early hydrogen bombs] representatives of the physical and medical sciences have been studying the problem. Observations on the distribution, origin, and nature of radiation have been made. The processes through which the human body is harmfully affected have been analyzed. The material collected, although far from complete, allows us to draw the conclusion that radiation resulting from the explosions which have already taken place represents a danger to the human race —a danger not to be underrated—and that further explosions of atomic bombs will increase this danger to an alarming extent.

This conclusion has repeatedly been expressed, especially during the last few months. However, it has not, strange to say, influenced public opinion to the extent that one might have expected. Individuals and peoples have not been aroused to give to this danger the attention which it unfortunately deserves. It must be demonstrated and made clear to them.

I raise my voice, together with those of others who have lately felt it their duty to act, through speaking and writing, in warning of the danger. My age and the generous understanding so many people have shown of my work permit me to hope that my appeal may contribute to the preparing of the way for the insights so urgently needed.

My thanks go to the radio station in Oslo, the city of the Nobel Peace Prize, for making it possible for that which I feel I have to say to reach far-off places.

What is radioactivity?

Radioactivity consists of rays differing from those of light in being invisible and in being able to pass not only through glass but also through thin metal discs and through layers of cell tissue in the human and animal bodies. Rays of this kind were first discovered in 1895 by the physicist Wilhelm Roentgen of Munich, and were named after him.

In 1896 the French physicist Henry Becquerel demonstrated that rays of this kind occur in nature. They are emitted from uranium, an element known since 1786.

In 1898 Pierre Curie and his wife discovered in the mineral pitchblende, a uranium ore, the strongly radioactive element radium.

The joy caused by the fact that such rays were at the disposal of humanity was at first unmixed. It appeared that they influence the relatively rapidly growing and relatively rapidly decaying cells of malignant tumors and sarcomas. If exposed to these rays repeatedly for a longer period, some of the terrible neoplasms can be destroyed.

After a time it was found, however, that the destruction of cancer cells does not always mean the cure of cancer and also, that the normal cells of the body may be seriously damaged if long exposed to radioactivity.

When Mme. Curie, after having handled uranium ore for four years, finally held the first gram of radium in her hand there appeared abrasions in the skin which no treatment could cure. With the years she grew steadily sicker from a disease caused by radioactive rays which damaged her bone marrow and through this her blood. In 1934 death put an end to her suffering.

Even so, for many years we were not aware of the grave risks involved in x-rays to those constantly exposed to them. Through operating x-ray apparatus thousands of doctors and nurses have incurred incurable diseases.

Radioactive rays are material things. Through them the

radioactive element constantly and forcefully emits tiny particles of itself. There are three kinds. They are named after the three first letters of the Greek alphabet, *alpha, beta, gamma*. The gamma rays are the hardest ones and have the strongest effect.

The reason why elements emit radioactive rays is that they are in a continuous state of decaying. The radioactivity is the energy liberated little by little. There are other elements besides uranium and radium which are radioactive. To the radiation from the elements in the earth is added some radiation from space. Fortunately, the air mass 400 kilometers high that surrounds our earth protects us against this radiation. Only a very small fraction of it reaches us.

We are, then, constantly being exposed to radioactive radiation coming from the earth and from space. It is so weak, however, that it does not hurt us. Stronger sources of radiation, as for instance x-ray machines and exposed radium, have, as we know, harmful effects if one is exposed to them for some time.

The radioactive rays are, as I said, invisible. How can we tell that they are there and how strong they are?

Thanks to the German physicist Hans Geiger, who died in 1945 as a victim to x-rays, we have an instrument which makes that possible. This instrument is called the Geiger counter; it consists of a metal tube containing rarefied air. In it are two metal electrodes between which there is a high potential. Radioactive rays from the outside affect the tube and release a discharge between the two electrodes. The stronger the radiation the quicker the discharges follow one another. A small device connected to the tube makes the discharge audible. The Geiger counter performs a veritable drum-roll when the discharges are strong.

There are two kinds of atom bomb—uranium bombs and hydrogen bombs. The effect of a uranium bomb is due to a process which liberates energy through the fission of uranium. In the hydrogen bomb the liberation of energy is the result of the transformation of hydrogen into helium.

It is interesting to note that this latter process is similar to that which takes place in the center of the sun, supplying it with the self-renewing energy which it emits in the form of light and heat.

In principle, the effect of both bombs is the same. But according to various estimates the effect of one of the latest hydrogen bombs is 2000 times stronger than the one which was dropped on Hiroshima.

To these two bombs has recently been added the cobalt bomb, a kind of super atom-bomb. It is a hydrogen bomb surrounded by a layer of cobalt. The effect of this bomb is estimated to be many times stronger than that of hydrogen bombs that have been made so far.

The explosion of an atom bomb creates an unconceivably large number of exceedingly small particles of radioactive elements which decay like uranium or radium. Some of these particles decay very quickly, others more slowly, and some of them extraordinarily slowly. The strongest of these elements cease to exist only ten seconds after the detonation of the bomb. But in this short time they may have killed a great number of people in a circumference of several miles.

What remains are the less powerful elements. In our time it is with these we have to contend. It is of the danger arising from the radioactive rays emitted by these elements that we must be aware.

Of these elements some exist for hours, some for weeks, or months, or years, or millions of years, undergoing continuous decay. They float in the higher strata of air as clouds of radioactive dust. The heavy particles fall down first. The lighter ones will stay in the air for a longer time or come down with rain or snow. How long it will take before everything carried up in the air by the explosions which have taken place till now has disappeared no one can say with any certainty. According to some estimates, this will be the case not earlier than thirty or forty years from now.

When I was a boy I witnessed how dust hurled into the air from the explosion in 1883 of the island Krakatoa in the Sunda group was noticeable for two years afterwards to such an extent that the sunsets were given extraordinary splendor by it.

What we can state with certainty, however, is that the radioactive clouds will constantly be carried by the winds around the globe and that some of the dust, by its own weight, or by being brought down by rain, snow, mist, and dew, little by little, will fall down on the hard surface of the earth, into the rivers, and into the oceans.

Of what nature are these radioactive elements, particles of which were carried up in the air by the explosion of atom bombs and which are now falling down again?

They are strange variants of the usual non-radioactive elements. They have the same chemical properties, but a different atomic weight. Their names are always accompanied by their atomic weights. The same element can occur in several radioactive variants. Besides Iodine 131, which lives for sixteen days only, we have Iodine 129, which lives for 200,000,000 years.

Dangerous elements of this kind are: Phosphorus 32, Calcium 45, Iodine 131, Iron 55, Bismuth 210, Plutonium 239, Cerium 144, Strontium 89, Cesium 137. If the hydrogen bomb is covered by cobalt, Cobalt 60 must be added to the list.

Particularly dangerous are the elements combining long life with a relatively strong efficient radiation. Among them Strontium 90 takes the first place. It is present in very large amounts in the radioactive dust. Cobalt 60 must also be mentioned as particularly dangerous.

The radioactivity in the air, increased through these elements, will not harm us from the outside, not being strong enough to penetrate the skin. It is another matter with respiration, through which radioactive elements can enter our bodies. But the danger which has to be stressed above all the others is the one which arises from our drinking radioactive water and our eating radioactive food as a consequence of the increased radioactivity in the air.

Following the explosions of Bikini and Siberia, rain falling over Japan has, from time to time, been so radioactive that the water from it cannot be drunk. Not only that: Reports of radioactive rainfall are coming from all parts of the world where analyses have recently been made. In several places the water has proved to be so radioactive that it was unfit for drinking.

Well-water becomes radioactive to any considerable extent only after longer periods of heavy rainfall.

Wherever radioactive rainwater is found the soil is also radioactive—and in a higher degree. The soil is made radioactive not only by the downpour, but also from radioactive dust falling on it. And with the soil the vegetation will also have become radioactive. The radioactive elements deposited in the soil pass into the plants, where they are stored. This is of importance, for as a result of this process it may be the case that we are threatened by a considerable amount of radioactive elements.

The radioactive elements in grass, when eaten by animals whose meat is used for food, will be absorbed and stored in our bodies.

In the case of cows grazing on contaminated soil, the absorption is effected when we drink their milk. In that way small children run an especially dangerous risk of absorbing radioactive elements.

When we eat contaminated cheese and fruits the radioactive elements stored in them are transferred to us.

What this storing of radioactive material implies is clearly demonstrated by the observations made when, on one occasion, the radioactivity of the Columbia River in North America was analyzed. The radioactivity was caused by the atomic plants at Hanford, which produce plutonium for atomic bombs and which empty their waste water into the river. The radioactivity of the river water was insignificant. But the radioactivity of the river plankton was 2000 times higher, that of the ducks eating plankton 40,000 times higher, that of the fish 15,000 times higher. In young swallows fed on insects caught by their parents in the river the radioactivity was 500,000 times higher, and in the egg yolks of water birds more than 1,000,000 times higher.

From official and unofficial sources we have been assured, time and time again, that the increase in radioactivity of the air does not exceed the amount which the human body can tolerate without any harmful effects. This is just evading the issue. Even if we are not directly affected by the radioactive material in the air, we are indirectly affected through that which has fallen down, is falling down, and will fall down. We are absorbing this through radioactive drinking water and through animal and vegetable foodstuffs, to the same extent as radioactive elements are stored in the vegetation of the region in which we live. Unfortunately for us, nature hoards what is falling down from the air.

None of the radioactivity of the air, created by the explosion of atom bombs, is so unimportant that it may not, in the long run, become a danger to us through increasing the amount of radioactivity stored in our bodies.

What we absorb of radioactivity is not spread evenly in all cellular tissue. It is deposited in certain parts of our body, particularly in the bone tissue and also in the spleen and in the liver. From those sources the organs which are especially sensitive to it are exposed to radiation. What the radiation lacks in strength is compensated for by time. It works day and night without interruption.

How does radiation affect the cells of an organ?

Through being ionized, that is to say, electrically charged. This change means that the chemical processes which make it possible for the cells to do their job in our body no longer function as they should. They are no longer able to perform the tasks which are of vital importance to us. We must also bear in mind that a great number of the cells of an organ may degenerate or die as a result of radiation.

What are the diseases caused by internal radiation? The same diseases that are known to be caused by external radiation.

They are mainly serious blood diseases. The cells of the red bone marrow, where the red and the white blood corpuscles are formed, are very sensitive to radioactive rays. It is these corpuscles, found in great numbers in the blood, which make it possible for it to play such an important part. If the cells in the bone marrow are damaged by radiation they will produce too few or abnormal, degenerating

233

blood corpuscles. Both cases lead to blood diseases and, frequently, to death. These were the diseases that killed the victims of x-rays and radium rays.

It was one of these diseases that attacked the Japanese fishermen who were surprised in their vessel by radioactive ashes falling down 240 miles from Bikini after the explosion of an hydrogen bomb. With one exception, they were all saved, being strong and relatively mildly affected, through continuous blood transfusions.

In the cases cited the radiation came from the outside. It is unfortunately very probable that internal radiation affecting the bone marrow and lasting for years will have the same effect, particularly since the radiation goes from the bone tissue to the bone marrow. As I have said, the radioactive elements are by preference stored in the bone tissue.

Not our own health only is threatened by internal radiation, but also that of our descendants. The fact is that the cells of the reproductive organs are particularly vulnerable to radiation which in this case attacks the nucleus to such an extent that it can be seen in the microscope.

To the profound damage of these cells corresponds a profound damage to our descendants.

It consists in stillbirths and in the births of babies with mental or physical defects.

In this context also, we can point to the effects of radiation coming from the outside.

It is a fact—even if the statistical material being published in the press needs checking—that in Nagasaki, during the years following the dropping of the atom bomb, an exceptionally high occurrence of stillbirths and of deformed children was observed.

In order to establish the effect of radioactive radiation

on posterity, comparative studies have been made between the descendants of doctors who have been using X-ray apparatus over a period of years and descendants of doctors who have not. The material of this study comprises about 3000 doctors in each group. A noticeable difference was found. Among the descendants of radiologists a percentage of stillbirths of 1.403 was found, while the percentage among the non-radiologists were 1.222.

In the first group 6.01 per cent of the children had congenital defects, while only 4.82 per cent in the second.

The number of healthy children in the first group was 80.42 per cent; the number in the other was significantly higher, viz. 83.23 per cent.

It must be remembered that even the weakest of internal radiation can have harmful effects on our descendants.

The total effect of the damage done to descendants of ancestors who have been exposed to radioactive rays will not, in accordance with the laws of genetics, be apparent in the generations coming immediately after us. The full effects will appear only 100 or 200 years later.

As the matter stands we cannot at present cite cases of serious damage done by internal radiation. To the extent that such radiation exists it is not sufficiently strong and has not lasted long enough to have caused the damage in question. We can only conclude from the harmful effects known to be caused by external radiation to those we must expect in the future from internal radiation.

If the effect of the latter is not as strong as that of the former, it may become so, through working little by little and without interruption. The final result will be the same in both cases.

Their effects add up.

We must also remember that internal radiation, in contrast to that coming from the outside, does not have to penetrate layers of skin, tissues, and muscles to hit the organs. It works at close range and without any weakening of its force.

When we realize under what conditions the internal radiation is working, we cease to underrate it. Even if it is true that, when speaking of the dangers of internal radiation, we can point to no actual case, can only express our fear, that fear is so solidly founded on facts that it attains the weight of reality in determining our attitude. We are forced to regard every increase in the existing danger through further creation of radioactive elements by atom bomb explosions as a catastrophe for the human race, a catastrophe that must be prevented.

There can be no question of doing anything else, if only for the reason that we cannot take the responsibility for the consequences it might have for our descendants.

They are threatened by the greatest and most terrible danger.

That radioactive elements created by us are found in nature is an astounding event in the history of the earth and of the human race. To fail to consider its importance and its consequences would be a folly for which humanity would have to pay a terrible price. We are committing a folly in thoughtlessness. It must not happen that we do not pull ourselves together before it is too late. We must muster the insight, the seriousness, and the courage to leave folly and to face reality.

This is at bottom what the statesmen of the nations producing atomic bombs are thinking, too. Through the reports they are receiving they are sufficiently informed to form their own judgments, and we must also assume that they are alive to their responsibility.

At any rate, America and Soviet Russia and Britain are telling one another again and again that they want nothing more than to reach an agreement to end the testing of atomic weapons. At the same time, however, they declare that they cannot stop the tests as long as there is no such agreement.

Why do they not come to an agreement? The real reason is that in their own countries there is no public opinion asking for it. Nor is there any such public opinion in other countries, with the exception of Japan. This opinion has been forced upon the Japanese people because, little by little, they will be hit in a most terrible way by the evil consequences of all the tests.

An agreement of this kind presupposes reliability and trust. There must be guarantees preventing the agreement from being signed by anyone intending to win important tactical advantages foreseen only by him.

Public opinion in all nations concerned must inspire and accept the agreement.

When public opinion has been created in the countries concerned and among all nations, an opinion informed of the dangers involved in going on with the tests and led by the reason which this information imposes, then the statesmen may reach an agreement to stop the experiments.

A public opinion of this kind stands in no need of plebiscites or of forming of committees to express itself. It works through just being there.

The end of further experiments with atom bombs would be like the early sunrays of hope which suffering humanity is longing for.

Appendix 4

MEMBERS OF THE UNITED STATES NATIONAL ACADEMY OF SCIENCES AMONG THE SIGNERS OF THE PETITION TO THE UNITED NATIONS

NUMBER: 104

C. A. Adams—Emeritus Professor of Engineering, Philadelphia, Pennsylvania

J. W. Alexander—Professor of Mathematics, Institute of Advanced Studies, Princeton, New Jersey

P. Bailey—Professor of Pathology and Bacteriology, Neuropsychiatric Institute, Chicago, Illinois

E. T. Bell—Emeritus Professor of Mathematics, California Institute of Technology, Pasadena, California

E. G. Boring—Professor of Psychology, Harvard University, Cambridge, Massachusetts

M. N. Bramlette—Professor of Geology, Scripps Institution of Oceanography, La Jolla, California

L. Brillouin—Professor of Physics, Retired, New York, New York

R. A. Brink—Professor of Genetics, University of Wisconsin, Madison, Wisconsin

A. F. Buddington—Professor of Geology, Princeton University, Princeton, New Jersey

M. J. Buerger—Professor of Mineralogy and Petrography, Massachusetts Institute of Technology, Cambridge, Massachusetts

238

R. K. Burns—Staff Member, Department of Embryology, Carnegie Institution of Washington, Baltimore, Maryland

H. E. Carter—Professor of Chemistry, University of Illinois, Urbana, Illinois

W. E. Coblentz—Consulting Physicist, Washington, D. C.

E. U. Condon—Professor of Physics, Washington University, St. Louis, Missouri

J. N. Couch—Kenan Professor of Botany, University of North Carolina, Chapel Hill, North Carolina

G. Dalldorf—Pathologist, New York State Department of Health, Albany, New York

H. Davis—Director of Research, Central Institute for the Deaf, St. Louis, Missouri

M. Delbrück—Professor of Biology, California Institute of Technology, Pasadena, California

M. Demerec—Director of the Department of Genetics, Carnegie Institution of Washington, Cold Spring Harbor, Long Island, New York

D. M. Dennison—Professor of Physics, University of Michigan, Ann Arbor, Michigan

Th. Dobzhansky—Professor of Zoology, Columbia University, New York, New York

J. L. Doob—Professor of Mathematics, University of Illinois, Urbana, Illinois

P. Doty—Professor of Chemistry, Harvard University, Cambridge, Massachusetts

L. C. Dunn—Professor of Zoology, Columbia University, New York, New York

J. T. Edsall—Professor of Biochemistry, Harvard University, Cambridge, Massachusetts

W. M. Elsasser—Professor of Physics, Scripps Institution of Oceanography, La Jolla, California

J. Erlanger—Emeritus Professor of Physiology, School of Medicine, Washington University, St. Louis, Missouri

K. Esau—Professor of Botany, University of California, Davis, California

L. F. Fieser—Sheldon Emery Professor of Organic Chemistry, Harvard University, Cambridge, Massachusetts

P. J. Flory—Mellon Institute, Pittsburgh, Pennsylvania

A. Forbes—Emeritus Professor of Physiology, Harvard Medical School, Cambridge, Massachusetts

R. M. Fuoss—Sterling Professor of Chemistry, Yale University, New Haven, Connecticut

J. L. Gamble—Emeritus Professor of Physiology, Harvard Medical School, Cambridge, Massachusetts

J. Gilluly—Geologist, United States Geological Survey, Denver Federal Center, Denver, Colorado

R. B. Goldschmidt—Emeritus Professor of Zoology, University of California, Los Angeles, California

J. P. Guilford—Professor of Psychology, University of Southern California, Los Angeles, California

V. Hamburger—Professor of Zoology, Washington University, St. Louis, Missouri

L. P. Hammett—Professor of Chemistry, Columbia University, New York, New York

H. S. Harned—Emeritus Professor of Physical Chemistry, Yale University, New Haven, Connecticut

M. Heidelberger—Professor of Immunochemistry, Rutgers, The State University, New Brunswick, New Jersey

J. Holtfreter—Professor of Zoology, University of Rochester, Rochester, New York

M. K. Hubbert—Chief Consultant, General Geology, Shell Development Company, Houston, Texas

M. R. Irwin—Professor of Genetics, University of Wisconsin, Madison, Wisconsin

J. R. Johnson—Todd Professor of Chemistry, Cornell University, Ithaca, New York

W. P. Kelley—Emeritus Professor of Soil Chemistry, University of California, Berkeley, California

E. C. Kemble—Professor of Physics, Harvard University, Cambridge, Massachusetts

R. H. Kent—Ballistic Research Laboratories, Aberdeen Proving Ground, Maryland

A. V. Kidder—Professor of Anthropology, Cambridge, Massachusetts

W. Köhler—Psychologist, Swarthmore College, Swarthmore, Pennsylvania

Izaak M. Kolthoff—Head of Department of Analytical Chemistry, University of Minnesota, Minneapolis, Minnesota

A. Kornberg—Professor of Microbiology, School of Medicine, Washington University, St. Louis, Missouri

W. D. Lambert—Professor of Geophysics, United States Coast and Geodetic Survey, Retired, Canaan, Connecticut

E. M. Landis—George Higginson Professor of Physiology, Harvard Medical School, Boston, Massachusetts

E. S. Larsen, Jr.—Geologist, United States Geological Survey, Washington, D. C.

S. Lefschetz—Emeritus Professor of Mathematics, Princeton University, Princeton, New Jersey

K. P. Link—Professor of Biochemistry, University of Wisconsin, Madison, Wisconsin

Leo Loeb—Emeritus Professor of Pathology, Washington University, St. Louis, Missouri

L. G. Longsworth—Member, Physical Chemistry, Rockefeller Institute for Medical Research, New York, New York

H. J. Lucas—Emeritus Professor of Organic Chemistry, California Institute of Technology, Pasadena, California

D. A. MacInnes—Professor of Chemistry, Rockefeller Institute for Medical Research, New York, New York

Max Mason—Mathematician, Retired, Claremont, California

W. F. Meggers—Physicist, National Bureau of Standards, Washington, D. C.

C. W. Metz—Professor of Zoology, University of Pennsylvania, Philadelphia, Pennsylvania

S. A. Mitchell—Emeritus Director, McCormick Observatory, University of Virginia, Charlottesville, Virginia

H. J. Muller—Distinguished Service Professor of Zoology, Indiana University, Bloomington, Indiana

M. S. Newman—Professor of Chemistry, Ohio State University, Columbus, Ohio

S. B. Nicholson—Astronomer, Retired, Mount Wilson Observatory, Pasadena, California

S. Ochoa—Professor of Biochemistry, New York University College of Medicine, New York, New York

L. Pauling—Professor of Chemistry, California Institute of Technology, Pasadena, California

A. Petrunkevitch—Emeritus Professor of Zoology, Yale University, New Haven, Connecticut

J. R. Pierce—Director of Electronics Research, Bell Telephone Laboratories, Murray Hill, New Jersey

D. Rittenberg—Professor of Biochemistry, College of Physicians and Surgeons, New York, New York

O. H. Robertson—Emeritus Professor of Pathology and Bacteriology, Stanford University, Stanford, California

A. S. Romer—Alexander Agassiz Professor of Zoology, Harvard University, Cambridge, Massachusetts

Karl Sax—Professor of Botany, Harvard University, Cambridge, Massachusetts

H. I. Schlesinger—Emeritus Professor of Chemistry, University of Chicago, Chicago, Illinois

P. A. Shaffer—Professor of Biochemistry, School of Medicine, Washington University, St. Louis, Missouri

H. Shapley—Paine Professor of Astronomy, Retired, Harvard University, Cambridge, Massachusetts

T. Shedlovsky—Associate Member, Physical Chemistry, Rockefeller Institute for Medical Research, New York, New York

David Shemin—Professor of Biochemistry, Columbia University, New York, New York

G. G. Simpson—Curator, American Museum of Natural History, New York, New York

B. F. Skinner—Professor of Psychology, Harvard University, Cambridge, Massachusetts

E. E. Snell—Professor of Biochemistry, University of California, Berkeley, California

G. L. Stebbins—Professor of Genetics, University of California, Davis, California

N. E. Steenrod—Professor of Mathematics, Princeton University, Princeton, New Jersey

S. S. Stevens—Professor of Psychology, Harvard University, Cambridge, Massachusetts

W. H. Stockmayer—Professor of Physical Chemistry, Massachusetts Institute of Technology, Cambridge, Massachusetts

A. H. Sturtevant—Professor of Genetics, California Institute of Technology, Pasadena, California

A. Szent-Györgyi—Director of Research, Institute of Muscle Research, Marine Biological Laboratory, Woods Hole, Massachusetts

K. V. Thimann—Professor of Plant Physiology, Harvard University, Cambridge, Massachusetts

E. C. Tolman—Professor of Psychology, Retired, University of California, Berkeley, California

M. A. Tuve—Director, Department of Terrestrial Magnetism, Carnegie Institution of Washington, Washington, D. C.

C. B. Van Niel—Herzstein Professor of Biology, Hopkins Marine Station, Pacific Grove, California

O. Veblen—Professor of Mathematics, Institute of Advanced Study, Princeton, New Jersey

M. B. Visscher—Professor of Physiology, University of Minnesota, Minneapolis, Minnesota

V. F. Weisskopf—Professor of Physics, Massachusetts Institute of Technology, Cambridge, Massachusetts

F. W. Went—Professor of Plant Physiology, California Institute of Technology, Pasadena, California

R. H. Wetmore—Professor of Botany, Harvard University, Cambridge, Massachusetts

R. C. Williams—Professor of Biophysics, University of California, Berkeley, California

D. W. Wilson—Professor of Physiological Chemistry, University of Pennsylvania, Philadelphia, Pennsylvania

O. Wintersteiner—Director, Division of Organic Chemistry, Squibb Institute for Medical Research, New Brunswick, New Jersey

S. G. Wright—Leon J. Cole Professor of Genetics, University of Wisconsin, Madison, Wisconsin

W. H. Zachariasen—Professor of Physics, University of Chicago, Chicago, Illinois

O. Zariski—Professor of Mathematics, Harvard University, Cambridge, Massachusetts

Books and Journals

Articles dealing with all aspects of the problem of nuclear weapons, war, international relations, and applications of nuclear energy for peaceful purposes can be found in the *Bulletin of the Atomic Scientists,* a magazine of science and public affairs published monthly (except during July and August) by the Educational Foundation for Nuclear Science, Inc., 5734 University Avenue, Chicago 37, Illinois.

Many interesting popular articles about nuclear energy have been published in the *Scientific American,* a monthly magazine published by Scientific American, Inc., 415 Madison Avenue, New York 17, N. Y.

The greatest easily available source of detailed information about some of these questions is *The Nature of Radioactive Fallout and Its Effects on Man,* a two-volume report of the hearings before the Special Subcommittee on Radiation of the Joint Committee on Atomic Energy of the 85th Congress of the United States, 27 May to 7 June 1957, United States Government Printing Office, Washington, 1957.

The following books may be recommended for additional information:

GLASSTONE, SAMUEL. *Sourcebook of Atomic Energy.* Princeton, N. J.: D. Van Nostrand Co., Inc. (2nd ed.), 1958.

Lapp, Ralph E. *Atoms and People*. New York: Harper & Bros., 1956.

——. *The Voyage of the Lucky Dragon*. New York: Harper & Bros., 1958.

Pirie, A. (ed.). *Fallout: Radiation Hazards from Nuclear Explosions*. London: MacGibbon and Kee (2nd ed.), 1958.

Schubert, Jack, and Lapp, Ralph E. *Radiation: What It Is and How It Affects You*. New York: The Viking Press, Inc., 1958.

Index

INDEX

250

INDEX

Poincaré, Henri, 33
Pollard, Ernest, testimony before
    Special Congressional Subcom-
    mittee on Radiation, 97
Polonium, 34
Population problem, 206
Powell, C. F., 159, 165
Price, C. C., 162
Priestley, Joseph, 171
Pugwash Conference, First, 159-160
    Second, 160

Rabinowitch, Eugene, Franck Re-
    port, 158
Radiation, biological effects of, 39
    cancer caused by, 82, 83-85, 92,
        99, 106, 147
    disease and, 77-111
    from cosmic rays, 40
    from natural sources, 40-42
    mutations caused by, 57-58, 67
    from wrist watch, 125-128
    genetic effect of, 49-76
    heredity and, 49-76
    life expectancy and, 93-100, 105
    Maximum Permissible Dose
        (MPD) of, 129-132
    mutation and, 56-61
    somatic effect of, 77-111
    Special Congressional Subcom-
        mittee on, report on hearings,
        112
    threshold dose of, 96-100, 107
    units of measurement, 39-43
    see also Fallout
Radiation sickness, 48
    acute, 78-80, 81
    in Hiroshima, 7
Radium, 34
    half-life of, 37
Radon, 34, 35, 36-37
Radioactive rays, cancer treatment,
    35
    disease diagnosis, 35
Radioactive substances, as a source
    of energy, 34
    half-life of, 36-39

Radioactive substances (Cont.)
    Maximum Permissible Concen-
        tration (MPC) of, 129-132
Radioactivity, 32-48
    discovery of, 33
    involved in a nuclear attack, 141-
        146
    see also Radiation
Radiocarbon, see Carbon-14
Radiocarbon dating, technique of,
    37-39
Radiothorium, 83, 92
Radon, 84
    half-life of, 36-37
Raman, Sir C. V., 163, 165
Rand Corporation, 200
Reichstein, T., 166
Research, 195-208
    applied, 198-199
    for peace, 195, 201-209
    for war, 199-201
Rider, Fremont, 217
Roberts, Arthur, 162
Roentgen, Wilhelm Konrad, 32-33,
    196, 227
Roentgen unit, defined, 39
Roosevelt, Franklin D., 157
    "Advisory Committee on Ura-
        nium" appointed by, 6
Rotblat, Joseph, 63
    quoted on nuclear war, 136, 141,
        142
    Russell-Einstein appeal signed
        by, 159
Rubidium-90, 44
Russell, Bertrand, quoted on dan-
    gers of thermonuclear weapons,
    158-159
    scientists' petition to UN signed
        by, 164, 166
Russell-Einstein appeal, 158-159
Rutherford, Ernest, 5
Ruzicka, Leopold, 166

Sachs, Alexander, 6
Sands, M. L., 162
Schomaker, Verner, 162
Schubert, Jack, 63, 64

252

INDEX